The Refra

Reframing a Better You

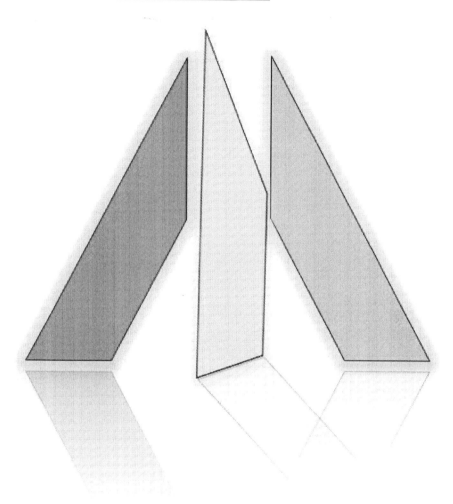

by Brian Maddox

What are you made of?

Copyright

Dedication

This book is dedicated to all the men out there, like me, who struggle to figure out why the nice guy arguably finishes last. I hope that "The Reframe" in turn motivates you to provide value in all your relationships and help create a shift in the staggering high current failure rate in marriages. I believe deeply that the content therein will benefit everyone, just like it benefited me in my own search for a true loving relationship. Thank you to all my readers for your ongoing support.

Additionally I wanted to give thanks to Marisa Jodoin & Sarah Wetyk for volunteering to edit my horrible spelling and grammatical errors. As an accountant grammar is not exactly a "core" skill I have mastered.

A special thanks is warranted to Amazon and CreateSpace for editing and distributing physical copies on an as needed basis. As well, Marisa Jodoin provided the remarkable cover page, giving the final product a much more professional appeal relative to anything I could ever muster.

Finally, I wanted to thank my parents for supporting me unconditionally. Through university and through all the crazy pursuits I seemingly randomly decide to pursue. You guy's probably won't agree with a lot of content in this book but I know you'll still support me anyway. – Love Brian.

The contents of building a better you:

Notes from the Author

"The Reframe" should be seen as a self-help book that is constructed in a way to build you up from your very foundations. It is broken down into three Pillars; Social, Health and Wealth. The bulk of the content lies within the Social Pillar as it is this section that is composed of the most convoluted, interesting and un-orthodox ideas.

My main motivation for writing this book originates from my own internal struggle to figure out why so many relationships fail. I wrote this book as an introverted accountant who had a house and a career and could not figure out why I was struggling to attract and maintain real loving relationships. During part of my courtship journey I realized some of the information I was receiving as feedback from my dating interactions would be largely beneficial to my male peers. After conducting and reading various books I realized there is not much strictly objective information to go by out there in the dating world today....at least from a male perspective.

This book is made for men. I would argue it could be useful for a woman but given the social stigmas, different social expectations and the fact that my point of view is that of a man I feel I would not do our fair female counter parts justice. With that disclaimer in mind, a woman might find this book both interesting and at some parts even humorous.

"The Reframe" is most beneficial for men aged between 21 and 38 who are pursuing or actively involved in relationships with women of around the same age group. For new relationships, mastering these three Pillars Social, Health and Wealth will enable you to draw confidence naturally from within and create attraction with the type of women you are actually interested in. For current relationships, understanding these three Pillars will enable you to ensure that spark keeps aflame with your significant other. Regardless of your Facebook relationship status examining these three Pillars will force you to reflect on things you can change within yourself for the betterment of both you and her.

Individually, we have no lasting effect on society's viewpoint on the subject of dating. "The Reframe" must rather than come from within ourselves. In relationships, the only guaranteed thing you can control is yourself. This is why "The Reframe" is "framed" as a self-help book. But the "reframe" is that if enough people start helping themselves we collectively can work towards starting a shift to better society.

So what does "The Reframe" really mean?

Reframing means changing the way you think about relationships. Why does the nice guy arguably finish last? Why is society wrong? Where is the disconnect? "The Reframe" examines key social traits you can utilize in all your relationships. This book illustrates ways to achieve a positive upward spiral, channeled from within, without regard for society's misguided views. Since we are changing the very ideas that are constantly reinforced by society we all have to actively keep working to reinforce these reframes.

I understand some people may not be empathetic towards what other people go through, with social conditioning limiting an individual's behavior in our everyday lives. As mentioned my motivations for writing this book is that I truly believe this will help the average Joe, like me, out there. Most of the Social content of this book was written while going out on a large number of dates and writing down commonalities that occurred. Generally this content came in the form of writing down what I was seeing and then brainstorming reasons why it was so similar, which greatly interested me given how every social interaction cannot be easily copied with all intricacies... yet these intricacies were fairly constant all the same. The Health Pillar is composed from research I used while achieving my own physical goals and then integrated back to the dating and social development framework. Lastly while being "wealthy" is not the main purpose of "The Reframe" I have found that being financially stable is a huge asset to achieving your goals. As a charted accountant by trade, I have compiled a few tips that I believe would be beneficial to the reader located in the Wealth Pillar of this book. Most importantly serving to illustrate how these wealth tips can lend themselves into achieving your Social and Health goals.

As a disclosure some of the Social content can be used for ``pick up`` or rather ``meeting women with no intention of ever dating them" but this book is not written with that intent. There is a critical difference between meeting a women or picking up a woman. The latter has the social stigma of "playing the game"... "gamy", if you will. This frame of mind can come across deceitful and fake as it comes from a "taking" mentality; offering no real value with "lines you don't mean" to "people you don't care about." "Reframe" each interaction with the mindset of finding a potential life partner and then you will find, like I did, that your intentions will become more genuine and sincere.

Recall the intention of this book is to educate and provide you with the tools to find a life partner you truly desire. Unfortunately you can read anything but never grasp the meaning of the words. In the words of Herbert Spencer (Victorian Era English Philosopher)... "The great aim of education is not knowledge... but action." Therefore in order to learn from this book you need to take action. The words written will fall dead on arrival without action reinforcing the content. Push yourself out of your comfort zone and don't succumb to your fear. This is an action book and without action you will not learn.

Why is society arguably so "crooked" when it comes to relationships? I acknowledge that parts of this book may go against social norms. However, I believe that when social relationships in the modern world aren't exactly working as intended (increasing trend of divorce rate) some rethinking/reframing is more than warranted. A reframe is needed.

In following this book I hope you will be able to improve your overall wellbeing and be cognitively aware that finding a life partner is not a passive process. I hope your betterment enables you to therein better others creating an undulating effect that elevates everyone you so happen to run into.

INTRODUCTION

Reframing relations starts from within. How you reframe is through the conduit of self-improvement. Social, Health and Wealth are the three pillars that make up the composition of this book. These three pillars were selected exclusively as these are the main areas where most people spend the bulk of their cognitive time and efforts.

Self-Improvement: The Imbalance

Estimated Waking Hours Allocated for the Average Joe (Assuming 8 Hours of Sleep):

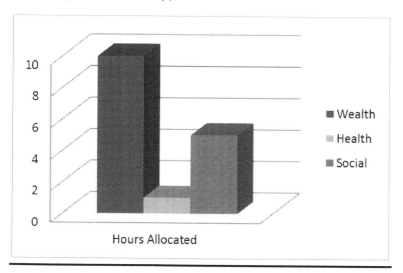

A basic allocation of 16 hours for the average person into the three Pillars is approximately ten hours to Wealth, five hours to Social and one hour to Health. Unfortunately, even with just a scarce five hours allocated to Social, we typically spend them not being very social at all (TV, Video Games, Twitter, Facebook, and Chores etc.)

It follows then, that due to societal norms, the average person has an abundance of waking hours allocated into the Wealth Pillar and a shortage of time allocated to Health and Social Pillars. Aggressive action to counteract this imbalance is required to ensure you have the maximum time available to pursue your avenues of growth and happiness.

This imbalance is no fault of your own but it is the root cause of why so many people are socially afraid/stifled and awkward. It is no wonder the average person is more likely to be afraid of public speaking then of actual life threatening situations.

Pursuing self-improvement via these three conduits (which are not mutually exclusive) will lead to an increase in your ability to attract and retain the type of women you are looking for. Not because you will actually have more to offer but because you will actually be happier/content just with being yourself. You will no longer feel like you need a partner just because the world states you ought to. Rather you will find yourself in a relationship because you genuinely want to.

The content in this book is an amalgamation of my own experiences and realizations through taking action combined with various credible external sources. That is you will find various underlying themes and ideas stemming from books like Dale Carnegie's "How to Win Friends & Influence People" and Stephen Covey's "The 7 Habits of Highly Effective People". For example, the first core skill in this book is Scarcity vs. Abundance, a concept initially brought forth by Stephen Covey but it is tailored and expressed under the specific context of dating and relationships. In fact many concepts in "The Reframe" you may be more familiar with outside of the dating realm. Appendix #11 is a bibliography of books I recommend you read, though none of them expressly relate directly to creating long term loving relationships. Furthermore, Appendix #12, are recommended YouTube persona's I also utilized to better convey my own ideas on long term dating. In particular one of these sources is Owen Cook from Real Social Dynamics (RSD). Please note Owen's material is short term in nature and he is a "pick up artist". That being said many of the core values headings and some content I mention in the first part of this book correlate well with RSD's more holistic generalizations. This is because many of Owen's original material and ideas also comes from more renowned famous authors like Stephen Covey. While RSD has branded itself as a more sex orientated, "gamy," short term view, sometimes utilizing shock and awe marketing tactics, there can be no denying the overlap between the two intentions during the initial phases of relationship building. Many of my journaled courtship findings correlate well with Owen's more holistic ideas despite this divergence of intention. Despite these disconnects you will likely find commonalities between "The Reframe" with these books and YouTube persona's listed in Appendix 11 & 12 throughout your reading as these are the sources of external information I used for research when trying to better express what I was noticing throughout my own courtship journey.

PILLAR #1: SOCIAL

The Social Pillar is divided up into four key parts. These four parts, respectfully are: Core Social Skills, Non-Essential Social Skills, Technology and finally Common Mistakes people are likely to make.

Social skills are the most important component in dating. Mannerisms, body language, vocal tonality and facial expressions are all critically important; however, these skills can only truly be taught and therein calibrated through taking action via repeated physical exposure and not through literature. For example, a book can tell you to sit up straight but it can't effectively show you how. Or a book could tell you speak with more authority and someone might honestly translate that into yelling all the time. Therefore the things that I will focus on in this book are the cognitive social concepts you can practice that will help you to understand why the average person behaves a certain way and why the average person fails to get the desired mate he or she wants, given the ever increasing trend in number of failed marriages. In fact the American Psychological Association states, "40 to 50% of married couples divorce in the United States." Statistics can be manipulated but there is no denying even optimistic sources would show at the very least an increase in the rate of divorced marriages in the developed world over the last 40 years.

How can we get that divorce rate back under control and stop this unfortunate increase in failed marriages?

This book argues that it starts from within. The first part of the social Pillar will start with core ideas I believe everyone should draw from regardless of whether your intent is picking up girls, dating/courtship and/or marriage. These 10 concepts are key in attracting, selecting and most importantly maintaining a healthy relationship. How far you decide to take the relationship is contingent on simply what you want in life at any given point in time.

The Ten Core Social Critical Components:

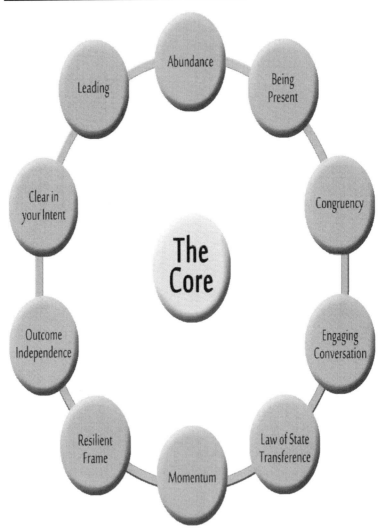

Each of these core social skills are all equally significant and are therefore presented in this book in no specific order. You will only be as strong as your weakest skill so prioritize accordingly.

S1.1: Scarcity vs. Abundance

Scarcity...Wait, what? Don't worry, this isn't an econ book, at least not until the Wealth section. So why should we care about scarcity and abundance when dating?

The initial concept of Scarcity vs. Abundance comes from Stephen Covey's, "The 7 Habits of Highly Effective People" where Covey argues that from the abundance mentality, "flows a deep inner sense of personal worth and security." Well the abundance mindset is important for appreciating others and coming from a genuine place in yourself it follows that it also plays a pivotal role in the dating world. Most crucially coming from the contrasted, "Scarcity" mentality, lends itself towards displaying traits of neediness, fear of loss and insecurity.

Stephen Covey further states that the scarcity mentality is a "zero-sum paradigm" of life. Coming from a place of Scarcity means in order for you to win someone has to lose. This is undeniably toxic in relationships. The only reason you should be in a relationship is so that both of you are "winning". Putting one of you above the other and then deciding to "compromise" to take turns to be the "winner" will not suffice in the long run. This give and take, bargaining mentality if you will, has no place in generating meaningful human interactions.

Scarcity and Abundance in the context of dating should be viewed in regards to the amount of women you see every day. This doesn't mean having sex with multiple women but it does advocate "shopping around". Too many people in today's society fail to breakout of their comfort zone and end up dating someone who is convenient as opposed to the right one. They think they've "found the one" when really they haven't "found" anything because they haven't even branched out from their extended social circle. Essentially, this is just leaving the duty of finding your significant other up to fate and hoping that this "friend of a friend" is the right one for you. Instead take action, know what you are looking for. A potential life partner isn't something to leave to chance. Finding a life-long partner is the most important decision you will ever make because it has rippling effects on so many other decisions down the road (traveling, children, retirement, general everyday happiness, etc.). Don't leave it to auto-pilot. Don't leave it to chance.

How do you know if you are coming from a scarce mentality?

If one is too scarce with women they tend to be seen as needy. Neediness is actually the most common turn off that continually reared its head when I went around asking women what their three biggest turn offs were. Scarcity tends to blow your emotions out of proportion; when you need her more than she needs you. A victim of scarcity typically is controlling, insecure and constantly worries about what their partners are up to. A guy who calls & texts to keep checking up on his partner but only during times when she is out with her friends is the typical symbolic demonstration of neediness, not protection, and can be originated back to the idea of scarcity. You value her so much because she is everything to you but ironically this fear of losing her can actually drive her away. This fear lends to the belief that there is potentially someone else out there that she will think is better than you are. You should believe that you are the best partner for her simply because you love her the best and if she does actually decide to find someone else that is out of your control. Frame it as her loss and move on. The easiest way to do this, even while "blinded" by love, is to always maintain some degree of abundance.

Coming from a place of scarcity will make you come off unattractive to the person you are interested in because you need her to react to you in a certain way. You <u>need</u> a specific reaction from her. Instead, if you came from an abundant mindset, this effect becomes naturally diluted as you don't genuinely care as much about how she is likely to react to the things you say. Clearly you do not want to strive for bad reactions but you won't take it personality or rather defensively when they happen.

Additionally from scarcity also stems putting women on a pedestal which is another topic altogether. You care about what she thinks more than what you think. You cave to her whims instead of telling her what you actually think and feel. In the long run a woman doesn't want you to be fake & constantly putting her ahead by sacrificing what you want. A women will eventually want a guy with his own identity and backbone who can assert himself. Not just be a cheerleader to sit by her side and praise her. In the long run this pedestal paradigm would cause resentment for both of you because you are compromising your genuine identity at your expense but she doesn't know that. This miscommunication will cause resentment because subconsciously you feel like you are making all the sacrifices when the reality is you are actively choosing to make these sacrifices that she is not even aware you are making. Putting a woman on a pedestal, as weird as it seems, does make you fake and this insincerity will stem to eventual relationship failure.

So why does Abundance work as a solution to Scarcity?

Mainly because of dilution. Initially, if you are just meeting someone for the first time, it's the basic dilution effect of that there is more "fish in the sea". Abundance works in that you can be comfortable in being genuine because you can focus on being yourself & listening to her as opposed to being constantly afraid and working to keep her interested in you. It's far better to be yourself than to worry about not losing someone or trying to find devious ways to capture their interest. <u>Scarcity blinds your objectivity in relationships.</u> Remember your goal is to find the best partner for you. Not the first one. The idea of Abundance comes in to help benchmark one women to the other. Not only does this ensure you are picking and falling in love with the best woman for you but it also makes you less socially awkward and stifled. You won't have trouble with figuring out what to say when you don't care as much what she thinks of what you are saying. Most importantly, with abundance you won't just fall for the first girl who bats an eyelash and throws a wink your way. This is pivotal in being able to choose someone who you actually enjoy being around and not just anyone who showed interest in you at a time when you didn't have many options.

The hard part in combating scarcity is actually in how you foster abundance when you find "the one" after "shopping around". You have to remember females in general, especially attractive females, get hit on multiple times a day (depending on where they go and the occupations they have pursued) and ultimately will maintain some degree of abundance themselves. Society however, has a double standard for women who date multiple men so that abundance is somewhat constrained by the fear of society's judgement. That social judgement is neither here nor there, but you should be aware of it. So back to fostering abundance in a relationship... obviously you don't see other women, you don't play jealousy games, but you put something else as your primary purpose. Too many men will suddenly put the lady "first" in their life, sacrificing other things, which on the surface sounds romantic and cute but in actual practice is horrible. This is the time when men "change" and become "controlling, needy and jealous" and is made even worse because she won't understand that it's because you value her too much. This sudden change in behaviour is incomprehensible/random and can't be communicated easily as the man isn't even cognitively aware of it. This is partially because he subconsciously feels "he choose her and limited himself in some way" when she didn't really have to choose him given that she will always be surrounded by some degree of abundance, at least until she gets older and/or less physically attractive.

To avoid scarcity after finding the woman you like, you have to put something other than her as your primary focus. That something else could be constant self-improvement. You can make it a book, the gym, your body, your job, your knowledge, a specific skill set, your "cooking"... but the idea of constant self-improvement is something you can always rationalize and something your significant other can support you in.

The two ways to ensure scarcity does not affect you is either by staying single (which is actually recommended until you are resourceful enough to lead and ensure you come from a place of abundance when you decide to become "exclusive") or to ensure your primary focus is not your significant other. You provide value because you don't need anything from anyone and become self-reliant with yourself. She can depend on you and you can depend on her though you shouldn't need her. By dating from a place of abundance you will know what you want out of a relationship and be more able to find someone who supports you and the goals/aspirations you want at any given time.

Tips about Scarcity:

- When searching for your potential significant other aim for roughly 2-3 dates a week with different women. If you do that for 2-3 months you will have at least 16-36 references. These benchmarks will enable you to know the type of person you react well to... be she a thrill seeker, a book worm or someone who also believes in self-improvement and reads self-improvement books. You will start developing a "type" and be able to draw out & develop common patterns among all the women in your interactions. Only then should you start dating one weekly while still seeing others (let her know you are still looking but think you see something with her). So, you might ask how you manage to get 2-3 dates a week. Two ways: <u>Cold approach</u> - approaching strangers you are attracted to, and <u>online dating</u>. If you have extra money and are tight for time, paid online dating is an easy way to go. This lets software filter down to women with "bachelor degree and no children but wants children etc." I highly recommend doing both. Cold approaching strangers and conveying attraction builds up so many social skills you need if you want to constantly exhibit high quality confident male traits while naturally beating down your ego.

- Never be afraid to just get up mid date and say, "I don't feel like we have something here." Sticking around when you know it won't work just screams either neediness or being gamy. You are not doing the lady any favors by wasting her time or yours.

- Frame generating abundance as making sure you are going for the right woman for you; not just simply shopping around. Shopping around by itself can be easily taken out of context and can have negative connotations due to its easy association to "sleeping around". Do your due diligence and search for the right girl for you. Examining who you really want to date, instead of just who is around, benefits both your time and that of the ladies equally. Coming from a state of scarcity and settling for anyone does a long term disservice to everyone involved.

<u>Challenges for abundance (pick one depending on your current dating situation):</u>

1. Try to date 2-3 woman a week for 3 months. These references will quickly enable you to map out the types of traits you are looking for in a potential suitor. Additionally, this allows you to genuinely express yourself with confidence to the people you so happen to meet. This steady stream of dates will also enable you to form your identity. Not only will you see commonalities in what your dates are saying but you will quickly come to understand the types of topics you also find interesting which will likely lead to self-discovery.

2. Put something else besides your significant other's happiness as something you are striving to achieve. Your primary purpose should be something you want. Not something you think she wants. This doesn't mean putting her aside in so much as putting yourself first. Putting yourself first will directly result in bringing everyone else up who has the benefit of knowing you; especially your significant other.

S1.2: Being Present

This core skill was originally going to be called "listening" until I realized that for a core concept it had to go deeper than that. Being Present is a very simple, holistic core competency that stems from basic Zen ideology. The idea of being present is simply not living in the past or thinking about the future. Think about just being in the moment. Not thinking about anything else except what is in your surrounding environment. "Realize deeply that the present moment is all you ever have." – Eckhart Tolle, Author of "The Power of Now".

Be careful. Don't take being present to the extreme where you are constantly indulging, partying and not caring about the future. Or alternatively failing to keep in mind the lessons you have learned in the past. You should always be "preparing" to enable yourself to be present (which in itself is a conundrum) and utilize the wisdom you learned from past experiences to enable you to know when it's a safe environment to give into the present.

Why does Being Present matter in dating?

It matters because you become more mindful of the situation around you. You become more aware of how the person is behaving, making you more likely to be genuinely interested. You can better calibrate to the stimulus around you, making you appear witty, fun and spontaneous. By being present you can more readily identify how you are feeling at the time allowing you better mastery of your emotions which lends itself strongly into "The Law of State Transference" that will be mentioned later. This ability to identify your emotions further transcends in your ability to detect an ego which is critical in your ability to destroy this aforementioned ego.

Why is that effective though?

Because the status quo of competition is a random guy who "numbed" his wits with beer in order to "man" up and say hi to the lady he thinks he likes because she's wearing a low cut shirt. While that above sentence is a hit on all the indulgent, non-self-improving average guy even the smartest, driven people don't stop and smell the roses and often end up looking like slave's to their own electric devices. In the wise words of Ferris Buhler, "Life moves pretty fast. If you don't stop and look around every once in a while, you could miss it."

Being present also lets you shake off rejection if you are in the early stages of finding a relationship. This present state allows you to move on to the next potential partner with little to no emotional baggage from previous failings. Fixating on rejection will effectively force you to live in the past whereas being present enables you not to linger with regards to any recent "failings." Reframe any rejections by assuming the point of view that the sheer act of approaching someone without the crutch of beer while being congruent with your intent of conveying attraction is success all in its own; regardless of how the person you are interested in reacts to it.

If you are generally present already you would discover that most people find you fun, outgoing and high energy. Chances are if you are generally coming from a future point of view you then most people would say you're successful, smart, quiet, and introverted. Remember neither mind frame is bad. The key here is balance and knowing when to pull what you want from each mindset based on current environmental stimulus. Generally you will find yourself in the mind frame you are most comfortable in; which therein correlates to the one society pushes you in. For example, being an accountant, most of my cognitive hours are spent planning and mapping out the future both for work and for my personal life. By default I don't have to react to the present unless there are "fires" to put out which, in of themselves, will likely occur because of lack of planning. Therefore I personally lend myself to and am more comfortable with the future mindset.

Unfortunately, this comfort can create an "ego" which means you will begin to identify with your default mindset and jerk away from the other. Suddenly, you might start getting jealous of people who spam "YOLO" and take off backpacking around the world for a year. You might even become pretentious and look down on anyone who doesn't plan for their future. Or you might just run from the present by constantly keeping yourself busy for the future. You might venture off into playing video games to kill time (killing the present) or play video games that simply foster progression so as to keep you in that forward looking mindset. Avoid favoring one mindset above the other. Do not praise one above the other. They are both uniquely important. The man who plans for a fire might purchase a fire extinguisher ahead of time but the man who lives in the present isn't afraid to pull the pin and aim it.

The main reason why being present is so critical is because many men simply aren't. This simple skill is a competitive advantage in the world of relationships. Just by being mindful, listening to what others are saying and contributing to conversation will actually set the stage for being more socially aware. This social awareness will set you above others, as well as your previous self, and therein make you a better catch for your potential significant other. How many times do you hear the "he never listens to me" theme from the fairer sex? While planning for the future is a worthy endeavour, you have to also enjoy the moment and cultivate the wisdom of deciding when to toggle between present and future from the experiences of the past. The journey beats the destination, especially when the final destination for all of us is death.

Achieving being present sounds easy and it is with practice, but in reality it is difficult because you actually have to cognitively think about it.

Tips on How To Practice Being Present:

- React immediately to stimulus around you and be secure in the absolute knowledge that whatever you say is genuine with how you are feeling at that time based on that stimulus.

- Free word association games with just a pen and paper are an easy way to become present & in the moment. These games can also be practiced alone therefore alleviating any forms of social anxiety.

- Practice mindless tasks. Force your thoughts only at the one mindless task at hand and remove all others.

- Brief meditation periods are suggested. It allows you to take a break from the constant stimuli around you, identify a sense of nothingness and therein filter out all the past events and future plans. Meditation is technically the most symbolic form of practicing a mindless task.

- Practice social games with friends such as "categories" where one of your friend's lists a category and you have to take turns in a circle coming up with nouns ASAP that fit under this category. Other fun games that help express yourself in the present moment, like charades, will also serve to bring the present & carefree side of you out. You can utilize these games as a reference point to be honest with yourself if you struggle with being present in the moment. Fear of playing these games is one of the strongest forms of ego preservation and/or social anxiety.

Challenges for Being Present:

1.) Narrate in your head (or out loud if you're brave enough) what you are doing while you are doing it. Obviously narrating out loud is contingent on your environment. This identifies the thoughts in your head and will make you acknowledge just how many "unpresent" thoughts trickle into your mind subconsciously. A first time interaction with an attractive lady you are head over heels for is not the time to be thinking about some future plans. Embrace the now. It's yours.

2.) Meditate 5 minutes a day every day. You could even do this in the shower. Breathing is a mindless task, simply focus on breathing. This will relax you enough to give you the opportunity to appreciate your current environment.

S1.3: Congruency

Stephen Covey talks quite a bit about "congruency" in his book, "The 7 Habits of Highly Effective People." But what exactly is congruency? Words to associate congruency in the dating framework would be authentic, genuine, sincere and honest. Interestingly, Owen Cook who as mentioned in the introduction is affiliated with Real Social Dynamics (RSD), largely encourages others to practice being genuine and congruent. It should be extremely fascinating to most of us that a "pick up artist" practices & preaches these traits. However, these traits are nothing new. In fact, Dale Carnegie cites being sincere several times in his classic masterpiece "How to Win Friends and Influence People." From modern effective Pick up Artists to older highly influential works being genuine will always be recommended when building meaningful relationships.

Do you ever hear women say I want a genuine guy? Well this is where congruency comes in. Congruency in the terms of dating, as Owen Cook expressly states in various YouTube videos, is an "alignment of your thoughts, words and actions." To be congruent you are really just being yourself. The reason why this is tough in practice is society often barrages you with feedback saying you are not enough. Women often fall prey to being fake even more so than men because of the aggressive marketing tactics in today's world. In fact this book, which preaches self-development, ironically could be taken in the context that your current self is not enough. The act of self-improvement can be an admission that you are not good enough currently. Owen Cook recommends that you have to "reframe" that feeling into an "I am already awesome and am just on a path to making myself more awesome." This reframe is also recommended by me, which is why I am quoting it. Remember while this book's intention is long term focused being genuine will work in all your relationships both in the short run and the long run.

Do you want to know the secret in relating to people? It's easy. Relating to people is obtained through being true to yourself and how you are feeling at that time. How to gain attraction is to take it one step further through expressing what you are feeling using that congruency as a conduit.

To take this out of the dating context think of the most popular comedians or YouTube authors. Do they feel fake or authentic? The best YouTube material will make you laugh when the artist laughs, etc. This is done through being authentic, genuine and ultimately congruent. Like being present, congruency facilitates the Law of State Transference which will be mentioned later.

Congruency doesn't have to be confidence.

Wait, what? Do you mean I don't have to be confident to get the girl?

No. All you have to do is be yourself and embody the emotion. If you are nervous, say you are nervous. "You're the first girl I've talked to tonight." Don't pretend to be cocky with "Hey Girl. You're a 9 and I'm the 1 you need," if you are feeling nervous as hell!

I was told always to be high energy when I meet someone new, is this true?

This is true, in general, but it can be exhausting. Coming in high energy is a good thing as long as it is genuine with how you are feeling. The idea behind being "high energy" is that you should be slightly more animated, excited, and engaged than whoever you are talking to before they started talking to you. This will make people want to subconsciously talk to you since you are temporarily providing better positive emotions to the interaction. A potential pitfall with focusing on being high energy is that you could be focused on generating high energy out of yourself instead of trying to relate to your date! Worse, it means that every time she sees you she will expect you to be high energy. This could result in a relationship where she feels like you aren't who she thought you were... and let's be real, you probably weren't. Women can succumb to the same thing especially when they are in a high stimuli environment like a club. The main reason why a women might flake on you when you thought you had something special is because she might have been in a different emotional state. She might be really sociable, bubbly and fun at the club because she is intoxicated with alcohol, loud music and positive feedback from other men at the bar but her day-to-day life is actually the complete opposite and she feels like meeting you outside of that environment would just be too weird/awkward.

The general rule of thumb is that you should try to come in with higher energy than whatever the potential suitor's energy level is currently at... but only with respect to how you are feeling. If you are tired don't pretend to be high energy. Most of the time women can tell and it comes off try hard or conversely, "creepy" ...and believe me, "creepy" made the top 3 on the "Turnoff List".

To be successful at congruency you have to readily express your thoughts, words and actions together in line with what you are feeling. This makes people understand your behaviour quicker, relate to what you are saying faster and makes them feel at ease around you because they understand why you are there. Basically, congruency assists people in deciding quicker what your overall personality is like. The quicker someone can get to know you the quicker they become comfortable around you and this comfort is required for attraction to build.

So why aren't men naturally Congruent?

Incongruence only occurs as a defense mechanism when you are not allowing your real self to be vulnerable. If you aren't being your real self then there is no real "pain". This again isn't your fault, the culprit is social conditioning. What incongruence is serving to do is protect your ego. "She didn't reject me, she rejected my pick up persona." This is because men fear rejection and their ego wants to protect itself. This comes from society's view that you were rejected because you weren't good enough for her or did something wrong. You need to change this mindset. While incongruence protects your true self from getting hurt you need to realize that when a woman rejects you, she barely knows the real you anyway. How can she know how great you are? How much value you provide? How much better you are than what you were before? How can she know from only an opening line about all the experiences you went through to make you the man you are today? In short, defeat the undermining defense mechanism of incongruence by realizing and firmly believing that she is not rejecting you because she can't possibly know you. Furthermore, by being congruent you display that you are confident and unafraid of being judged by those around you. By extension the extent of your congruence can be the barometer of your confidence.

Remember, while congruency does not necessarily equal confidence it does mean you are confident enough with who you are and how you are feeling. The act of admitting you are nervous to a stranger but taking the act of approaching her, making yourself vulnerable and conveying interest is confident. So, in fact, congruency implies confidence even when it's expressly contrary to the symbolic word confidence has come to mean. It is not very often you can be "confidently nervous" and feel like the interaction has a chance to succeed, but it does simply because you embrace your underlying emotion and are not afraid of it.

Dr. Seuss had this one right; "Today you are you, that is truer than true. There is no one alive who is youer than you". I challenge you to accept yourself and you will find that simply being genuine goes extremely far in building attraction. A girl doesn't want the perfect guy, despite what one would logically conclude. Rather she wants the guy who is perfectly okay with himself.

Tips on How to Practice Being Congruent:

- Walk up and tell people what you are feeling. i.e.: "I don't know what to say to you but I just knew that I'd regret it if I didn't take a shot and at least say Hi!" Alternatively, the opener can just be: "Hey, I'm feeling (insert whatever you are feeling)."

- What you can't fix, you feature. You can actually leverage your insecurities to a competitive advantage by embracing them, i.e.: If you are balding don't fight it... accept it. If you have a foreign/regional accent, embrace it. It's unique and it's you.

- If you are not feeling high energy don't pretend you are. Go to places like bars/coffee shops/malls where being relaxed is more expected. Or you could stay in and work on other hobbies and other self-improvement actions instead. Tailoring the venue to your energy level makes things easier and more natural; however, do not use this as an excuse to stay in.

- In general, listening to upbeat music on your way to any social setting is an easy way to get your energy level up and get your mind ready to have a good time.

Challenges for Congruency:

1.) Every time you go out at the beginning of the night just walk up to someone you are attracted to and tell them how you are feeling. Oddly enough this is a low risk opener that society thinks is a high risk opener. Really you are reverse engineering society's view that men shouldn't talk about emotions so instead you come off better than your competition because you are doing something they would probably never do (even the naturally confident men).

2.) Write out the insecurities you are likely to lie about to a stranger and figure out how to embrace those insecurities instead. For example, if you like Lord of the Rings but feel it's a little "nerdy," and Lord of the Rings comes up in conversation, you shouldn't be afraid to say, "this is kind of weird but I love Legolas in the Lord of the Rings and always wanted to take up archery after watching it!" Reframing insecurities and embracing them is talked about in great detail in the insecurity/Health section. Just like women, most men also have to figure out ways to deal with physical insecurities.

3.) If you are already in a relationship ask your girlfriend if she can tell when you are being genuine or fake. A woman has a much easier time reading a man than even he thinks; especially a man who holds nothing back and embraces the value-giving "sun" mentality (discussed later). Make sure to always be yourself and don't compromise your identity for anything. She is seeing you for a reason so be yourself.

S1.4: Engaging Conversation

For some reason us men always feel like we will run out of things to say, especially on those first few interactions. Relax, this happens to everyone... especially when you are out of practice because, quite frankly, you don't know what she will find interesting. And that's just fine.

The primary reason you can't think of things to say is because you are likely filtering yourself. Lower the bar. Whatever you say is good enough. While the right words and sentence structure might be important when you're writing a book it is not important when you are interacting with a woman. Women pick up on how you say things, why you are saying the things you are saying and the emotions behind it. When it comes to communication, body language, smiling and the emotions behind your words are infinitely more paramount than the actual words you say. This rings even more true in higher energy environments like clubs.

In general, don't use canned material. Avoid using rehearsed lines, not because society sees them as "gamy". But instead don't use canned material because canned material doesn't work in the long run. You will actually get bored saying the same things over and over again. Moreover canned material inherently comes off fake and therefore makes you incongruent with your personality. Instead of seeing canned material as a way to get a woman to react a certain way you should be using topics to generate emotions you want out of yourself. On the other hand, there may be a line that you've used a million times, but you still find it entertaining so keep saying it! Why? Because that line is congruent with your personality. At the onset of a cold approach interaction it doesn't matter so much what she finds interesting, she would much rather discover what you find interesting or funny. This is the difference between value leeching and value giving and is difficult to learn without experiences or reference points. Adding value and demonstrating higher value will be mentioned later. There is never one line that gets a woman to melt in your hand and there shouldn't be. If something is too easy it holds little to no value.

Instead of the traditional idea of canned material identify overarching topics you find interesting. If trying to elicit humor from yourself talk about things you laugh at. If you want her to be interested in the things you like, talk about something you are passionate about.

I would note that polarity and rollercoaster theory (discussed later) is a key way to express yourself, enthral your potential partner and help them remember what you are saying so they can choose to jump on "hooks" you left earlier. These "hooks" are simply topics that were briefly added into the conversation naturally. A basic example would be:

Male: "So what do you do for a living?"

Female: "I am a professional photographer and I actually just got back from Brazil for work."

With this conversation you can either follow up on photography or Brazil or the general theme of travel. She brought up the "hook" of Brazil probably because she wants to talk about her trip. However, you just have to pick one category, and then the remaining unpicked categories are hooks you can remember and leverage off of when the conversation slows down. This mindfulness also conveys that you are genuinely interested in her since it shows you are listening. Remember though, don't be afraid of pauses. Silence can be extremely effectual in telling a story. In fact, often times, each word in a sentence carries more weight if you say less of them.

In short, content doesn't matter. Talk about what you find interesting. If she's not reacting to what you find interesting that's just fine. You're just fine. You possibly just aren't meant to be together. For some reason every guy has an ego that says he can get every girl and win every fight. Do you really want to get every girl? Akin to Mr. Darcy in Jane Austen's Pride and Prejudice I can barely tolerate half the people (woman included) I have ever met. Always be willing to walk away. If you are adhering to the idea of Abundance, having enough things to talk about becomes very easy because you won't be judging the things that come out of your mouth before you say them. Becoming un-stifled also leads to more "in the moment" reactions, making you more present and conveying a sense of confidence because you truly believe what you are saying has value.

Tips on Never Running Out Of Things To Say:

- Lower the bar. Talk about things you know are interesting to yourself. Not what you think she might find interesting. Cut yourself some slack. You won't really know what she finds interesting when you just met her!

- Don't write down things to say. This just makes you robotic, not present or congruent with how you are coming across to your potential partner.

- Believe that whatever you say has value just because it comes from you. Reframe yourself to believing that she will be better off by having just met you, which she probably will be if you are constantly self-improving and are coming from a value-adding mindset.

- Go out to a social setting before going out on your date or to the club. This could be the gym, grocery store or just to the mall to shop around. You could even get ideas from your Facebook or Twitter feed as long as the topic that is currently trending interests you.

- Don't think ahead of what you are saying. Don't have an agenda. Be present in the moment. Build the track of the conversation one rail at a time without planning where the train will eventually be headed.

- Storytelling exercises – Telling specific stories about important exciting experiences in your life is a great way to make you a more interesting conversationalist. Additionally, they will be unique and she will not have heard them before.

- Don't shy away from the trends everyone is talking about in your social media. I know it's not original, but everyone is talking about it for a reason. This means it's likely the woman you are attracted to may have an opinion or thought on the common thread. Ladies, in general, are often more socially aware than the average guy so if you are struggling, pick something "trending" that interests you and run with it.

Challenges to Help You Never Run Out of Things to Say:

1.) Talk to someone you already talk to on a regular basis, like a close friend or family member, and notice how easily conversation flows. Then try to replicate this flow with a women you don't know. If you are still struggling to find things to say, determine if it's your own filter (what you say isn't good enough) or if you are still talking about things you think interest her instead of the things you know interest you. It takes two to make conversation flow; if your interests don't align don't be afraid to eject yourself and move on.

2.) The more you go out the easier it is to find things to say because you are already out in the world interacting with people in a talkative state. If you are behind your desk all day talking to no one it's difficult to all of a sudden just turn on a congruent talkative state. Therefore when going out to a social venue try to go out to smaller social settings beforehand to get you in a more socially expressive state.

3.) Identify the things that interest you. Usually if you are living in the moment it's a reflection of how you are currently spending your "free time". You could go to the local book store and look at the section headings of all the book genres and write down the categories you are genuinely interested in. Then identify the reasons why that category might be important to you. You have now just constructed a customized list of conversation threads that you are genuinely interested in.

S1.5: Law of State Transference

As referenced a few times in this book already the Law of State Transference plays a key role in determining how your interactions are likely to play out. The Law of State Transference is simply whatever emotion you are currently feeling is transferred to those around you. Think contagion, or with all the recent zombie hype over the past half a decade, think zombies. Instead of calling this core competency "Contagion" which could have been easily taken out of context I decided to use the term "Law of State Transference." This phrase originates from RSD via Owen Cook; however, it is additionally taught indirectly in most standard sales training exercises.

So why do sales employees learn about this Law, indirectly or otherwise?

It's taught through most sales training exercises as most companies want their sales employees to be passionate about what they are selling. This passion or excited state is what drives sales. People are more receptive to someone who truly believes in their product and genuinely believes your life will be better off with it. The effect of the Law of State Transference on others is really a reactionary barometer of how much you are expressing your congruent state.

But why are people more receptive to emotions instead of cold hard logic?

Why is someone more likely to buy something from a passionate salesmen instead of a disengaged one? Interestingly, a paper from the University of Parma, in Italy by Giacomo Rizzolatti and Laila Craighero, contend that it is because of "mirror neurons". These neurons subconsciously effect our emotions. Mirror-neurons are imitation neurons which primarily evolved for survival. For example if one monkey saw a tiger and started to run in fear it would automatically trigger the other monkeys to run in fear even without the other monkey's having to physically see this tiger. Rizzolatti and Craighero argue that there is an additional presence of an echo-mirror neuron which mediates speech perception. While I am not exactly doing their scholarly article justice basically this speech perception neuron _could_ explain why people respond more to how you are saying your words instead of the actual logic of the words you are saying.

To take the idea of mirror neurons in the dating world, if you're feeling depressed or sad it's likely that the woman will pick up on it and also start feeling worse than she was before because it's draining her energy.

So what emotions should you bring into your interactions if you want to best utilize the Law of State Transference?

The three best "positive" emotions that seem to catch easiest with other people are happy, excited (fun), or scared. Sharing an emotion literally makes her relate to you emotionally. That is you are connecting on an emotional level. The thing about State Transference is that it's very easy to do. All you have to do is be congruent with how you are feeling (so the intended audience is more receptive), believe that what you are saying has value (it's interesting to you so therefore it's interesting to them) and express it accordingly. While being "scared" might not be seen as a positive emotion it creates positive responses in those around you when you express that you're scared (making yourself vulnerable). Ultimately, being scared, is only positive when there is no actual life threatening situation... which contrasts directly with what your body is telling you when you finally decide to approach that woman you are really taken with. Your heart races, palms start sweating, and adrenaline starts kicking in....are you going to battle to the death or have you finally decided to be the tenth guy to ask her if she wants a drink?

Similar to how the Law of State Transference increases the likelihood of a sale it works just as well for making others more receptive towards you. If you are excited and are having fun other people will than want to be excited with you. A way to measure the type of emotions you give off is if people find you approachable in a public setting. Do people ask you to take their picture? Do women ask you to dance when you are on the dance floor and having a good time? Positive people want to be a part of positive things, so the more positive and happy you are the more you will attract other positive people. This Law of State Transference can actually help illustrate charismatic qualities which most suitors would find appealing.

In order to radiate these positive the emotions, you first have to get yourself in that emotional state. Therein lays the difficulty. The hardest thing about State Transference is that you can't fake being happy, excited or scared for a prolonged period of time. Therefore, in the medium to long run, it is argued the Law of State Transference requires congruency.

So it follows then how can you make yourself genuinely happy, excited or scared?

Interesting enough, you can actually force it. As William James, the "Father of American Psychology" and author of "On Vital Reserves, The Energies of Men: The Gospel of Relaxation" famously stated,

"Action seems to follow feeling, but really action and feeling go together; and by regulating the action, which is under the more direct control of the will, we can indirectly regulate the feeling, which is not."

Dale Carnegie, in "How to Win Friends and Influence People", further argues, "Happiness doesn't depend on outward conditions. It depends on inner conditions. Everybody in the world is seeking happiness – and there is one sure way to find it. That is by controlling your thoughts." So if you want to transfer positive emotions to your partner "force yourself to think happy thoughts."

Smiles are the simplest form of State Transference. It puts people at ease, expresses your happiness, leading to other people expressing that they are happy too ... effortlessly. Why do you think so many women say they want a man with a nice smile? And since you can't control your natural smile.... as long as it is genuine your smile is "nice" enough. In Dale Carnegie's wise words, "The value of a smile costs nothing but can create much. It benefits those who receive, without diminishing those who give." Always be smiling.

Later we will discuss an advanced topic that associates back to The Law of State Transference: Merging Groups. Introducing people to each other automatically makes you the leading person in the current situation. The dominant person in any setting has an amplifying effect on the Law of State Transference. As everyone's emotions are currently cascading, especially in a bar or club, the dominant person's emotion carries the most weight.

Tips on Utilizing the Law of State Transference:

- Before meeting a date or going out to the club first surround yourself with things that make you feel happy, fun and outgoing. The Law of State Transference doesn't just work on people around you but it also works on you as well, so harness the energy around you and funnel it at the person you are attracted to.

- "Think Happy Thoughts." Remember that William James reference. There is a reason I am quoting him more than 100 years after his death. The more positive you are the more positive people will want to be around you. When you are extremely positive you will find yourself repelling negative, overly critical people. Being able to regulate your emotions internally is the core of self-reliance. You effectively become the source of emotion instead of reacting in response to it.

- The more confident you appear with an emotion the more likely it is that people around you will respond in turn to that expressed emotion. If you are shopping at a mall and say "fire" out loud to yourself nothing will happen, except for maybe a few weird looks. But if you shout "Fire!" and point with panic on your face like you actually believe there is a fire, you would probably incite panic.

- Once you practice State Transference it becomes easier to figure out what emotions you are feeling, why you're feeling them and how you can make yourself feel better. Often times when I am feeling nervous in approaching someone I would just tell them that I am nervous. A woman has never replied with, "No you're not"; most women take you being nervous as attractive 1) Because it means you think they are attractive and 2) Because you were man enough to voice your emotions to a relative stranger in a world where men saying their actual emotions still has shameful connotations.

- Everyone has bad days. You are allowed to have them to. Use them to figure out why you are feeling out of it and how you can avoid it in the future. Never stop taking steps to help master the self-regulation of your emotions.

Challenges for the Law of State Transference:

1. Identify the things that make you happy, fun, excited and sometimes even scared. Immerse yourself with these things before you go out. Practice carrying this emotion into your interactions with women. Expressing those emotions automatically makes you congruent which will allow her to be able to be more comfortable around you.

2. Constantly focus on your emotions. This means being mindful. If something makes you sad or angry figure out exactly what it is. Don't lie to yourself. Don't passively wait for the emotion to subside. Even outside of the dating world figuring out what makes you unhappy will ensure a more successful life. I say successful because I only judge success based on how happy I am though everyone should have their own personified criteria/metrics for success. Mine just happens to be easy to achieve but hard to quantify.

3. Practice smiling. I once had a nickname of "smiley kid" in junior high. You can bet people had no problem approaching me. My challenge for you is to practice smiling in the mirror in the morning for 30 seconds each day. Admire how you look. Can you even look yourself in the eye for 30 seconds? Can you tell the difference between your natural smile and the strained smile you might make if you are forcing it? If you have the time you can even do other facial expressions in the mirror

just to show how you can give off totally different vibes and first impressions based on your facial expressions. The face can't lie as easy as the tongue. You would be surprised how far this little authentic body language can carry you in generating more meaningful relationships.

S1.6 Momentum

Momentum is specifically after the Law of State Transference as, in my opinion, momentum is a form of State Transference. The difference here is that no one on the receiving end can easily understand momentum which makes you not only come off exciting to your potential significant other but <u>mysterious</u> as well. Momentum for social interactions is simply feeding off of previous social interactions. Note that momentum will eventually be killed by ego. As you get more and more constant positive feedback you can become more and more arrogant, entitled or condescending. Therefore one's maximum momentum will only be limited by one's resistance to the generation of the ego. Enough constant positive feedback will give anyone an ego. However, the more you can pin your success on luck or other external things the longer you are likely to keep the social momentum rolling. This tactic will at least assist in maximizing the duration of one's social Momentum.

The only way to generate momentum is to take action.

The main reason momentum works so well is because it can't be faked. You can't sit at home and build momentum. You can only build the snowball by going out into the snow and start rolling. This means that the emotions conveyed from momentum are automatically congruent because it occurs naturally via taking action.

So what exactly are the natural emotions conveyed from Momentum?

The main one is a sense of entitlement. A sense of entitlement makes you feel that you have high self-worth and builds confidence. This increase in self-perceived worth makes you less stifled so you don't have to worry about what to say which enables you be more direct, present and genuine with the woman. Momentum also naturally implies abundance, simply due to recent positive social feedback you start feeling good about yourself. Feeling good about yourself automatically starts to make her feel that she should like you too. If you gain social momentum some women will even like you just because other women are also interested in you. Woman may even start asking, "Who is this guy?" "He can't be from around here?" Thus inferring as if the normal socially contrived rules no longer apply to you. The believe that people should like you because other's like you is a bit egotistical but generally you can get away with it when it's congruent up to the extent that you don't start identifying with the success of the temporary momentum. Group think is real in relationships and it can work in your favor. No on want's to get in the way of momentum and "kill the party" so people's individual judgement can be swept aside due to the preconceived notions of group think and the individual not wanting to risk being the "villain".

Tips to Maximize Momentum:

- The only way to gather momentum is by taking action. Momentum is out of your control which means it happens naturally and is always genuine. This perceived congruency means people are likely to be much more receptive towards you simply because other people are trusting their friends/peers or your previous interactions judgement.

- Once momentum has started (and only after it has started) try to attribute the positive feedback to luck or another external source. This will help in delaying the association of the success to your ego's identity.

- Since momentum can't be contrived by sitting on the sofa, these tips are just to prolong momentum as much as possible. The only short-coming is if you are already naturally confident and have a high self-esteem you will develop an ego even faster. The quickest way to defeat an ego is to consciously identify it before you start wanting to defend it. This is an ongoing battle and should be thought about habitually.

- If you're having a tough time starting your "snowball", start small. Go to social venues and approach employees. At the gym, ask the guy at the front desk how to use a specific machine. At the mall ask a nice old lady for the time. These things, as small as they may seem, actually do start building the snowball. How far you can roll that snowball is contingent on how easily you balance your ego in its attempt to identify with the success.

Challenges for Momentum:

1. Say "Hello," "Thanks," and "Please" to everyone you see in your day to day interactions. Greet people with basic facial mannerisms and smiles. These things seem small but can start that snowball off in the right direction at a low risk of backfiring. No one rational is going to be mad at you for saying thank you or asking for help. This challenge should be never ending and automatic and won't be a real challenge unless you suffer from forms of social anxiety.

2. Determine if your success is feeding into an ego instead of fueling future success. Egos are unattractive to everyone around you, especially women, and will make

you subconsciously feel either defensive to things that don't really matter to you or like everyone is beneath you. Remember, "There is nothing noble in being superior to your fellow man; true nobility is being superior to your former self" - Earnest Hemingway (Nobel Prize Winner in 1954 for The Old Man and the Sea). Identifying that you have an ego actually starts tearing the ego's walls down. Realigning your identity with self-improvement actively reduces the ego since the act of self-improvement is the realization that you are not currently perfect. Another way that I personally use to realize I am by no means perfect, and therein combat the ego, is by having rolling annual goals so that by the time I die I make sure to have a dream or goal that is left unfulfilled. Well that may be a sad concept, without that one unfulfilled dream, I would not know what would drive me to the highest pinnacle of improvement. You don't have to be the best in the world at anything but you have to be better than what you were the year before.

3. Talk to the first people you see inside whichever venue you choose to start taking action. It doesn't matter what you say or conversely what they say to you. Remember you are adding value just by talking to them and not looking for any specific reaction or outcome from the seemingly "pointless" interaction. You will find these people will be the same people at the end of the night that give you that reassuring smile when a woman you were really into just blew you off.

S1.7: Assertive: Keeping a Strong Frame

Mastering this topic means you will learn to be assertive. For this topic first I need to explain what a "Frame" is. The concept of the frame itself is vague and various sources site different meanings. For the context of this book a frame is simply your identity with set boundaries. Therefore use the conceptualized idea of a physical picture frame as the perimeter of your identity with you in the middle. A strong frame is an assertive sense of self. This simply means being able to stand up for yourself and the things you like despite other people testing, teasing or challenging who you are or the views you have. What makes a frame strong isn't how opinionated or interesting your identity is but how you react to people testing your boundaries. The best way to hold your frame is to be unresponsive to the people who are aggressively attacking it. These people are looking for a reaction, which means you can't be defensive. Women will often test your frame subtly just to see if you are who you say you are. They will begin testing for inconsistencies, for example, you actually hate country music but you are at a country bar. When asked you lie and say you like country music. The lady might then ask you to name your favorite country musician and then you either lie again (if you can think of one) or shatter the frame. When a frame is built on too many lies it becomes exhausting just to maintain because your actively maintaining something that isn't authentic/genuine. In this way while lying is bad...you did it because you liked the girl and wanted her to like you too (good intentions). However, this means instead of being defensive with your frame you passively accommodated something into your frame that doesn't belong there. This is not exactly a strong foundation to build any meaningful relationship on. Lying in this context is an admission that you felt being yourself wasn't enough.

As illustrated above, the two major pitfalls most men fall in when attempting to keep a strong frame is getting defensive when your frame is challenged or being too passive that you let anything inside. If people say you are more defensive perhaps you are seeing aggression when none exists. If friends are saying you are too passive and have no clue who you really are, even after knowing you for a long time, then perhaps you are too accommodating or diplomatic.

The book The Art of War states, "Defense implies lack; Attack implies abundance." Reacting to other people challenging you means that you are not in control of the situation. Even defending yourself admirably still means only gaining what an "attacker" allows to give you. Remember, your potential partner is not attacking you. Reframe her challenge into her trying to get to know the real you better. Or maybe it's her hinting that she thinks you are not being true to yourself.

Conversely, and this is more for established couples, when a woman tests you typically she thinks you are capable of being better than what you are displaying. Other times society may put you in a stereotypical frame that you yourself may challenge to change or deviate from. Relationships have no constant dynamic. This is important to mention so we are aware that our frame doesn't have to be constant forever. You can add things, beliefs and incorporate changes as you grow and learn. Just make sure your partner is aware of these changes or she will constantly keep challenging you in order to keep an understanding of who you really are. She is not trying to undermine you. Just understand you better.

Why does having a strong frame matter?

It matters because it tells a potential life partner who you are and what you stand for. Are you the type of guy that normally introduces himself to strangers and is the life of the party or are you the thoughtful shy type that just had to say "hi" this time because you would have regretted it if you didn't?

It is difficult to explain how to build a frame, but to start, you need a vague path. Maybe in your specific set of identity traits you currently see yourself as a positive person who, lives in the moment, takes action and believes in ongoing self-improvement. From there you should be able to identify what you do that proves these traits are true and why you like doing it. The answers to the why you like doing the things you do need to be assertive. For example self-improvement is an easy trait to be secure with. Unlike many other traits it's not abstract so it is easy to explain **what** it is to yourself. Now **why** do you like working on improving yourself? Is it because you like seeing progress? Does it make you feel like you are accomplishing something? Determine the best answer that you believe and ask yourself how would you react if someone did aggressively challenge it? Obviously the idea of "self-improvement" is easy to defend because no one reasonable would likely challenge you for saying you are actively in the pursuit of making yourself better. If someone did you could either ignore it, or just restate why it's important to you and that maybe it's not for everyone. For example, "I just like being able to look in the mirror and know what I am doing with my life and gauge how far I have come but yeah self-development probably isn't for everyone." If that same someone persists then the best course of action is to excuse yourself and walk away, they probably aren't worth your time, and it is highly likely they are fishing for a reaction. Some people might not think self-development is important because they have such a strong ego that it won't let them accept that maybe they should try to grow. An ego will always attempt to defend itself in all parties involved. To recap, be able to identify the key things that make up your identity, what they are in a non-abstract relatable way, why you like doing it and how you can defend (without being defensive) any of those answers.

The overall purpose of this book is reframing your views and point of view on relationships given society's views on relationships aren't quite working as intended. Like reframing your views on relationships you can also reframe points of views on your immediate surroundings. Reframing; however, does not mean reframing your identity. It means reframing your mind set or point of view about a specific situation. It is not a gimmick or "gamy" tactic you are using on someone. Instead, you are simply changing your own interpretation of your external environment, i.e. reframing what people are saying to you in an effort to keep moving the conversation forward and reverberating those fun, positive, uplifting emotions you want to be associated with. The quote "There is no such thing as failure, only feedback" by Robert Allen is a reframe as it changes the point of view of failure. For the purpose of dating, reframing should be used as a tool to remain positive and upbeat despite possibly running into someone who leaves you feeling worse about yourself. Remember you don't know how any conversation will go before you approach someone which is what makes relationships so beautiful yet scary.

The most powerful frame and default "reframe" is to always make sure you are coming from a win/win mentality. This is arguably the most effective and easiest frame to maintain. It's very difficult for someone to attack you if you are genuinely trying to help both of you. You should truly believe that you approaching someone will make them better off in some way. You have to just be able to answer why someone would benefit by just meeting you. Maybe they will be happier, maybe they will learn something, maybe they will crack a smile or just maybe you will alleviate some of the tedious monotony in their day to day life for a short while. And who knows, maybe they will meet their life long partner. Coming from a win/win mindset that you truly believe in also means you will be less anxious when approaching a woman you really like. If you actually believe, deep down to your core, that you talking to her has the potential to make both of you better, then you are less likely to let the woman you really want to date slip through your fingers.

Reframing, when done correctly, is natural and smooth; this shift in point of view conveys overall confidence and the ability to think on your feet. It additionally illustrates that you are resourceful enough to persevere against an individual's somewhat unjust assault on who they think you are. Reframing, in hindsight, provides an avenue to evolve and become insightful about who you are.

Reframing should not be used to change who people think you are, but it is a tool you should master in order to be able to navigate through hard situations and challenges a potential life partner may throw at you. It means seeing the humor in situations and thinking about things in a different way that doesn't necessarily have to follow the narrative that the women is coming from. Reframing does not mean taking on a new personality.

Tips on Keeping a Strong Frame:

- A strong frame comes from a strong sense of self. This does not mean being the most interesting guy in the world. It means being able to assert yourself on certain things you relate to or believe in. Being strong does not mean being defensive or imposing your views on others. Being strong means being resilient to situational challenges. People will test your views and women should test your views especially if they are thinking about being in a relationship with you.

- People only have as much power as you give them. Don't let people tell you what should and shouldn't be in your frame. Disney's "Inside Out" is a great movie that entertains the idea that there are physical pillars that make up your identity. Watch that movie. What are your pillars? How can you affirm those pillars?

- Your identity will change as strong life events occur. Let it happen and embrace those changes. They are important to you for a reason so you'd better be able to relay to others why they are important to you.

- If you struggle with creativity then chances are you struggle with reframing your mindset when actively already engaged. Reframing correlates well with improv, however, improv relies on role play and is played out so that the audience knows that the actor is not truly congruent with whatever situation is thrown at the actor. I challenge you to try your hand at an improv class or at least go to a show and be cognitive of the reframes that happen throughout the evening. The trick here is to also remember that in real life situations you are not an actor putting on a show. The audience knows the actor is putting on a show. Don't be an actor when approaching that woman you like. Don't do yourself or her that disservice. Learn that the bar for your typical improv show is actually quite low, people just want to laugh and be in the moment. Expectations are lower because it's not rehearsed. Remember that, especially when contemplating using canned material.

Challenges on Keeping a Strong Frame:

1. Get a piece of paper and write down all the key identity traits that make you autonomous from other individuals. Now remove all the ones that have to do with a career or job. If this is difficult, think of the things you like to do; the bands or type of music you like, the things that take up your spare time. Be able to assert these hobbies or activities that make up your identity without being defensive or ashamed by answering the "what and why" questions as illustrated earlier. Stating why you believe the things you believe to someone else without shame or defensiveness is what asserting your frame truly means.

2. Determine if you are likely more defensive or passive. Ask the five people closest to you. They will tell you if you are feeling threatened when there is a challenge or if you are letting too many things inside your frame. This will act as a loose indicator to determine if you should be more or less assertive in your day to day life. If they don't know err on the side of passive as they would be able to tell if you are defensive. On the other hand if you are always defensive they may not be comfortable even answering the question truthfully.

3. If you are feeling bold, bring up politics at a family event. Simply observe who attempts to attack other people's identity/beliefs. Who shrugs it off with maybe humor and a smile? Who just nods their heads in agreement with everyone? Who just states how they feel in a "take it or leave it attitude"? After the event,

individually, ask each person why they choose to express their political views in a certain way. The person who states how they feel about the subject and doesn't argue with anyone is the person who you should try to emulate when keeping a strong frame in mind. Avoid emulating the person that tells other people they are wrong and tries to impose their frame on everyone else. Aggression is a fight or flight response and given that there is no immediate physical danger from discussing politics it could translate into the person being insecure about their own views. It also shows an overall lack of respect or empathy for other people's thoughts which needs to be avoided in almost all social settings, especially on a date with a potential partner.

S1.8: Outcome Independence

Outcome independence indirectly originates from the Scarcity vs. Abundance mindset Stephen Covey talks about. Covey mentions that, "the abundance mentality recognizes the unlimited possibilities for positive interactive growth and development, creating new third alternatives." That is abundance allows for outcome independence. In dating, outcome independence, simply means not having an agenda. Never go into an interaction expecting something. Expectations come across as neediness because you need people to react to you in a certain way. When it comes to human relationships you should remove the word "expectations" completely. Better yet, replace the word expectations with the word "appreciation". **Expectations** inherently "**takes**" for granted, while **Appreciation** inherently "**gives**" praise. When you approach someone you like, regardless if she responds energetically or if she tells you to take a hike, you need to be indifferent towards the reaction. Realize that some women will actually already be in a relationship, some will be busy and some just are not in the mood right now to talk to anyone. You can't control any of those things and therefore it should not matter to you that she blew you off. If it does bother you that means you have a self-image ego that is still not completely beaten down. I say completely beaten down because approaching strangers in an effort to elicit a date is not exactly ego friendly.

Pushing a good interaction to get a phone number, take her home or to another venue for a date should not matter to you. It doesn't matter how the end result plays out because social interactions contain too many unquantifiable variables that are beyond your control. You should be happy enough that the interaction was successful and that you were able to conquer both your social anxiety and ego simultaneously.

If you are getting feedback saying you are "pushy" or maybe even "aggressive" this means that you are superimposing your agenda on the woman. You need her to react a certain way and if she doesn't, you keep pushing for her to react the way you want using different tactics or social cues. Forcing someone to do something is not outcome independence.

Being free from outcome allows you to become un-stifled because you are not after anything from anyone. You are simply there trying to have a good time and possibly meet someone you can spend your life with. If you are still feeling unsure about what to say then you perhaps have "expectations" on how the social interaction should go. Expectations should only be used for hard quantifiable goals, not human relationships. The expected bar of success in this case is too high and you are likely too scared to fail so it hinders you from talking. This fear stems from outcome dependence. If you are not attached to how the interaction will turn out then you won't be scared to screw it up. This fear can be overcome by having an abundance of dates or alternatively, gauging your criteria of success by just being able to approach a stranger and evoke a conversation. Society seems to think that walking up to a stranger, genuinely conveying attraction and making yourself vulnerable is easy to do; however, most of society has actually never done it. Just to be clear to society, it's not easy. At some points I would even call it terrifying.

Conversely, you can also be outcome dependent if you are protecting your ego. To satisfy your pride you need her to like you and no other reaction will do. Defending your pride is a camouflaged tactic of the ego. This preservation of pride can only be overcome by identifying the ego using the tools aforementioned in the momentum section (S1.6), specifically under Challenge #2.

The caveat for outcome independence is that setting your success criteria to "low" can create an excuse for inaction. If your gauge for success is too low and occurs without effort then it is not making you more socially strong or savvy. You should want a certain goal or outcome but you are not attached to it. This means you want to approach with the mindset that she will like you but you won't take it personally if she says she is not interested. It is difficult to balance this conflict. On one hand, you do want a positive result but on the other, you want to be outcome independent. Indeed, the majority of this book is about self-development or even setting goals to measure progress, so how can you do that if you don't care about the outcome?

Don't fall into the trap of not caring at all. This is not the same as being outcome independent. Going up to women and making a fool of yourself because you don't care about anything is not achieving outcome independence. It instead achieves looking like a fool. Don't take outcome dependence too far. Instead view outcome independence as a way to remove emotion and dissociate from the result. So you finally got those abs? Embrace the positivity, but don't develop an ego with the outcome. So you just got rejected? Reframe it to learn from the failure and improve yourself in future endeavors, but don't take the rejection as a slight on your identity. Anger from rejection stems from the ego and simply not caring about anything is just a defense mechanism preserving it. Know the difference.

Tips on Outcome Independence:

- Differentiate outcome goals from outcome dependence. You should want the overall interaction to go a certain way and to strive for it but you can't be impacted by the outcome (good or bad). This is difficult because the more you strive for the outcome the more you will expect a certain (positive) result. You should come from the frame of always giving it your all but expected nothing back anyway. You don't need anything back. This is a cornerstone for adding value which will be discussed later.

- Being outcome independent means giving up a certain amount of control. If you generally like to feel in command of the situation, you will have trouble with this. This need for control should be viewed as a sign of ego preservation. A strong ego always favors control and fears change. Focus on letting go of any outcomes, good or bad.

Challenges for Outcome Independence:

1. Determine if you have an agenda when meeting women. You should plan for the outcome you want but be indifferent toward what actually happens. To determine if you do have an agenda when meeting strangers, identify if your mood is affected positively or negatively from new social interactions. This can only be done by socializing with strangers. No short cuts. If the result of the interaction makes you feel negatively impacted than you may care too much about the outcome. Strangers shouldn't be able to influence your emotions if you expect nothing from them, especially when you are the one who engaged them.

2. Distinguish between outcome goals from outcome dependence. Remember, you want the interaction to go a certain way but you can't be impacted by what actually happens. Things outside of the social spectrum such as education, money and health need to be result oriented or outcome dependent as that is the innate

motivation to succeed. For outcome dependence in social settings you have to forgo this innate motivation. In order to replace this motivation you could replace outcome independence with the goal for self-humor. Therefore the only reason you have to approach people is to entertain yourself and if you find the outcome of the social interaction entertaining then it worked. This is the best way to maintain motivation when you can't care about how the outcome goes. As long as you are having fun meeting new people and saying whatever you find amusing at the time then you will no longer care about how the outcome unravels.

3. Outcome independence can be achieved automatically if you come from a state of abundance. See the Challenges and Tips in S1.1 to help achieve a state of abundance which will directly relieve the pressure to have a good outcome. The end result will automatically mean less to you because you have so many more opportunities for different outcomes. The effect is therefore naturally diluted. You won't take "failing" as harshly when you have many other avenues available for success.

S1.9: Transparency – Being Clear

If you have achieved Congruency (S1.3) than you likely are already being largely transparent and genuine. Transparency could logically translate into eliminating mystery from our interactions completely, which is not recommended. Rather a better term that is less likely to be taken out of context is making sure you are "transparent in your intent" in your relationships. The term "Clarity of Intent" originates from Real Social Dynamics. Clear in Your Intent in the dating context means being obvious in your intention with the woman you like. Do you want to just have fun and party and try new things and meet new people? Or do you want a man to women relationship? This is more challenging than you think because society, in general, conditions both sexes to be fairly indirect with their sexuality. Women can get shamed and labeled "promiscuous" (or worse) by society if the woman starts being proactive and shows interest to just one or two men in a night. Meanwhile men get positive feedback from the same interaction, benefiting from the double standard but only if they "succeed" given that social success is measured just by not receiving a negative reaction.

If you ever get that "creep" feedback from a woman that means you were not clear in your intent. She doesn't know what you want from her because you don't know yourself. Or if you do, you are afraid to express it. Regardless, this "wishy washyness" comes off as being creepy. It should be noted that being clear in your intent does not have to be sexual. Women can find you just as creepy if you are passive and not approaching anyone.

Think of clarity of intent as you coming in and making it very plain to everyone around you what you are about. The key to achieving clarity is to make sure your intent is not divided. You can have multiple intentions, like having a vague intention of just partying or having fun while also having the intention of meeting a potential life mate, as these are both positive intentions. A true division of intent occurs when your **positive intentions** are mixed with **preventive intentions**. Preventive intentions are generally things like fear, nervousness or "what if" scenarios. When the positive intentions amalgamate with the preventive intentions then, as Owen Cook from RSD states "it's like having one foot on the gas and the other on the break." This leads to disjointed "thoughts, words and actions" because you are juggling too many thoughts at once. This division leads to being stifled which in turn makes you lag behind the interaction despite your best efforts to be present.

The average male's intent is constantly divided. Below is a short listed example of common intentions I picked at random that can flood your mind when you are contemplating meeting/ approaching someone you are interested in:

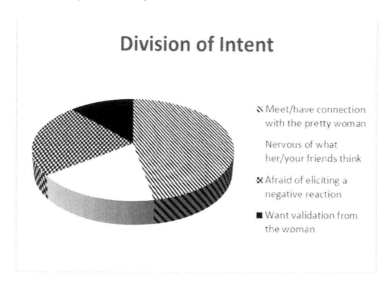

Division of Intent

- Meet/have connection with the pretty woman
- Nervous of what her/your friends think
- Afraid of eliciting a negative reaction
- Want validation from the woman

As previously mentioned, this division of your intent can carry negative connotations. But why do you come off as a "creep" if you're probably just nervous about approaching someone new?

Let's paint a scenario. You've been thinking about approaching this women all night but she is constantly surrounded by a group of friends. You don't want to put her on the spot or potentially get turned down in a group setting, so you finally seize your moment when you see her leave to use the restroom. It's perfect, she's alone and you've gained the "courage" to introduce yourself. <u>Wrong!!</u> She probably feels ambushed, she's planning on returning very soon to those same friend's you were too nervous to meet in the first place, plus she was on her way to the restroom for a reason. Not exactly painting the picture for long term success, are we?

Women are likely to deem you as creepy because they don't know you are nervous or afraid (how could they if you don't clearly show it) so it feels like you are jittery, unsure or up to something. Think of it like the lady wants to see why you came up to her and she is trying to uncover what your intentions are. If you aren't clear how can she know? How could she have a clue what you are about or what your intention is if you don't?

Another way to tell if you are too divided in your intent is if the women are viewing you like you are trying to sell them something. Think a stereotypical used car salesmen selling a potentially unreliable product. When the salesmen is being purposely vague or dodgy than it becomes "clear" that the car he is selling is probably not in your best interest to buy. In the social setting it means you approached but don't believe in your product, the product in this situation being you. You don't come off as nervous and cute but instead shady and up to something. Chances are if you are eliciting this type of reaction it's because you are trying to sell something and the lady's aren't buying it. Instead remember you want nothing from the women directly, they don't have to "buy" anything from you at all, you should simply want to introduce yourself, that's your intent.

In both of these cases the woman doesn't know why you are approaching them, so make it transparent what exactly you are about. If you are interested in her, make it clear. If you are just trying to have fun and let loose, make it clear.

To help identify if you are unclear in your intent determine if you are being stifled when you meet someone. Does conversation come naturally in the interaction? If not perhaps it is because you are too worried about what people around you think. This worry typically means you are not 100% committed to the primary intent of just conveying interest. Focus on the action you want to take and it is likely to be a self-fulfilling prophecy with how you see the interaction going.

Another indicator of not being clear in your intent is if women put you in the "friend zone" when you want something more. This means you did not meet her with the intention of wanting to date her in the first place. Maybe the fear of what she might think if you mentioned your attracted to her made you guarded. Unfortunately, by not being true to your intention and not making yourself vulnerable she thinks that you just want to be friends. This also conveys a degree of low self-confidence since you are unwilling to be honest with how you feel around her. The onus is on you to make it clear; not for her to figure it out. The longer you wait the more blindsided she will be. The friend zone kills any potential for attraction as the woman does not want you to be interested. She would value a male friend more than just another guy who lied about how he felt just to be around her more. Worse, if she does date you after you were "friend zoned" it is likely only because she was unable to find someone else which means you were just "convenient" and could perversely be viewed as a type of consolation prize. For dating being clear in your intent that you are looking for a man to woman relationship is your best bet to ensure the relationship starts off on the right path. The most effective, yet scary way to do that is to walk directly up to her, say "hi" and that you are interested getting to know her. The worst she can say is the neutral, "I have a boyfriend." Interestingly this seemingly neutral reaction will actually make you feel better just because you had the courage to walk over without hesitation to convey your intention exactly in the way you wanted to.

Tips For Being Clear In Your Intent:

- Keep it simple. The simpler the intention, the easier it is to be clear in it.

- Keep it positive. Make sure your intention has a positive tone.

- Focus on your intention and pick one achievable action that provides the best probability for the desired outcome. The more direct the better. Indirectness correlates with manipulative, unsure behaviour.

- Don't have intentions just for dating. Have a general goal you want accomplished by the end of the day. Having constant goals means you have an objective which will ultimately propel you forward each and every day.

Challenges for Being Clear In Your Intent:

1. Decide what your intention is before going out. Write it down and say it aloud over and over again for thirty seconds. This may sound odd. However, you would be surprised how certain situations will suddenly make you afraid to be yourself and show her exactly why you decided to introduce yourself. This reinforcement of repeating your intention will prevent you from forgetting your intention during a period where your body starts feeling stressed and anxious. The subconscious intent I used when meeting people was "I

am approaching you because I want to have a meaningful relationship with someone I am attracted to." The more you believe you are a high value man the easier it will be to approach strangers you are attracted to.

2. If you know someone you can trust, share with them your intention. They can help keep you accountable. This is challenging because it makes you vulnerable to that person as they know what you are genuinely after. However, if you start drifting away from your intent it means your friend will be there to let you know. Finally, a good friend will make sure there is no rock to hide under or excuses to make when you fail to make your intention known, whereas your mind may subconsciously hide the truth if only to protect an ego.

S1.10 Leading

I was struggling to decide what the 10th key core social skill would be. After again, going through countless source material from dating to finance from Dale Carnegie to various pick up artist material, it became clear that leading was much too common to be ignored. The ability to take the lead is crucial in giving your relationship an opportunity to reach its full potential. This topic could be seen as a little dated or misogynistic even but by the end of the topic I think you will agree that leading is significant in a relationship. Perhaps the chauvinistic taint on the subject itself is why so many men fail to learn how to lead. Leading in a relationship, loosely means, assuming the onus for everything that happens at any time, good or bad. If traffic is bad when you leave to go to the lake on your weekend getaway date it's your fault. It's not fair and it's not supposed to be. Take on the responsibility for your actions and take responsibility for your actions as a couple. However, this does not mean taking responsibility for her individual actions.

Leading is attractive because it means you hold yourself accountable for things greater than yourself. It also means the burden of any outcomes are on you. This means the women can remain carefree and loving regardless of how things turn out. She also knows you are human and that it's not fair to put the burden on yourself as a couple but she will love you for it because you will do it anyway. Additionally, because you are the leader in the relationship this means you always have an idea where you are going and have an invested interest in how things turns out. This means you will naturally care about all the activities you guys do as a couple. Too many men eventually stop caring about the events they do as a couple and just go to relationship autopilot. They mechanically follow and do whatever the girlfriend, fiancé, or wife wants to do. Leading forces the man to be cognitive for events you go to together which means that you will automatically start looking forward to these events, making them overall better and genuinely getting excited about them. The more excited you are about any event the unsurprisingly more present and cognitive you will be when you are there which means you will automatically get more out of any event. This powerful leading upward spiral phenomenon should not be ignored. Society has made it so that so many men are afraid to fail. Fear of failure translates to fear to lead and ultimately renders inaction which means the woman has to pick up the slack in order to try to move the relationship forward.

Leading when you've just meet a woman can be difficult as you don't have any indication on the types of things she likes to do which means you will likely be unsure what the best course of action is. When in doubt, lead anyway, do the things you want to do. Instead of saying "Do you want to go somewhere to eat," Say "I'm hungry, let's eat" then be spontaneous, and go somewhere with the full assumption that she will follow. Even better, pick a place to eat you haven't tried before as this will additionally access a more excited state in yourself which she will likely pick up on.

Come from the frame of mind that the only wrong action is inaction. This frame assumes you are rational. Make the best decision you can based on all the information available at that time and just go with it; with no "Plan B". Recall division of intent, just having a "Plan B" makes the odds of "Plan A" falling through increase. Pick a direction and start walking and if it turns out to be the wrong direction, as more information becomes clear, don't be afraid to change course. Don't be stubborn. Dating is supposed to be light and fun so if "Plan A" fails there are no long term consequences. Ultimately, the best plan of action is just to throw all your cognitive power into making "Plan A" succeed and if it fails reframe it so you can keep it going in some other way. Reframing is a way to keep leading forward in the face of difficulty, don't just pack it in and give up easily.

Leading in relationships has its perks. If you struggle with leading you would do well to remember these perks. Leading means going where you want to go. Which means you can start planning events you actually want to do as a couple. Want to go camping and fishing this weekend? Be passionate about it, be excited and if you picked a good significant other, she will be excited as well and want to be with you. Want to just go alone with the guys for the weekend? Then do it. Leaders naturally don't need permission, they should know what their followers and partners want and listen to them but it doesn't mean waiting & prohibiting taking action until everyone agrees.

Leading means the woman needs to trust in you. If she doesn't trust you ask yourself why. Do you not trust yourself? Did you screw up in the past? Is she leading and maybe doesn't think you are as capable as she? Let her know you got this. Let her know you care. Let her know you are okay with failing and leading the wrong way. If she still won't give up the reins tell her the positive leadership upward spiral loop and how you will take the onus for all good and bad outcomes. She doesn't need that responsibility she has enough things on her plate.

If she doesn't trust you chances are she is leading. This can actually be changed by direct action. Tell her you want to lead. Tell her you want to help influence what you guys do as a couple. Surprisingly, she will likely be relieved, as if it was an issue the whole time you didn't know existed. Conversely, she may not be relieved if she has developed an ego attached with control. If you feel that she is actively undermining your ability to lead simply tell her so. Maybe it just means you are not compatible as a couple.

Are you afraid of leading? Can you lead yourself just fine outside of the relationship? Perhaps your significant other is making you doubt yourself. If you are already in a relationship does she berate you when you screw up? Does she try to move past it? Or does she constantly bring it up? Don't be afraid to tell her how you feel. Fear of leading leads to inaction and this is why so many men in long term relationships take the passenger seat. While the significant other may feel like she is "winning", remember a successful relationship shouldn't have a loser. In the worst of cases this fear can effectively emasculate you. You are afraid to lead because of the negative reinforcement from your significant other which "leads" to you not taking an active interest in your relationship. Women, deep down, do want a man of action, even if they "attack" you when you fail. Tell her how her reactions to your failed attempts at leading are effecting you. Voice your emotions. Actively communicating to her that you feel emasculated to the point of inaction will make her think about how she is treating you. You've signed up to be on the same team so you best start acting like it.

A strong tip and highly recommended activity is ballroom dancing. This is an easy way to see if there are any trust issues with you being in charge. It also aligns with self-improvement (given it's a new skill set) and you can pull out these moves at any/all important social functions. Suddenly work parties, clubs, fundraisers and most importantly weddings you will be seen as one of the "best male dancers" on the floor because you decided to take some time and learn how to dance. You will also know promptly if you suffer from poor posture because any good dance instructor will let you know rather abruptly. As briefly mentioned, much of the communication in relationships is driven by body posture, especially at the onset of any interaction, therefore it is critical to master your composure or you may lose the woman you are attracted to before you even open your mouth. You will also gain confidence at social functions because you won't shy away from dancing like most of your peers will. Lastly, saying you took dancing lessons has, in my experience, almost always been met with intrigue and sparkling eyes. A man who knows what he is doing is attractive. A man that knows what he is doing on the dance floor makes him automatically notable because it is so uncommon these days.

Leading doesn't just have to take place in a dating relationship. It is also critical in just leading yourself to where you want to be in life and the goals you want to achieve. First make yourself accountable for your actions and then you can start making yourself accountable for all group actions you happen to be a part of. If you can't even make yourself accountable for your own actions then it is no surprise the lady isn't letting you lead.

Leadership will happen in various roles throughout your life; not just in dating. Leading will happen naturally when you have a child or when you are in a position of management with direct reports. Lead through example and empathy and not from a place of expectations. Leaders should offer value, not take value from their followers. Effective leaders lead by example. If your employees are failing initially it is probably because you are failing to lead.

There may come a time when you want to actively try to help someone around you become a better version of themselves. Perhaps your partner. For their own benefit, not yours. Often times, especially those closest to you will not want to hear it. They may feel like you are trying to change them instead, no matter how pure your intention. If you want to directly aid someone close to you with regards to self-improvement it is often best to act as though that particular characteristic were already one of their outstanding traits. This effectively gives them a "fine reputation to live up to, and they will make unusual efforts rather than see you disappointed." – Dale

Carnegie. So if you don't really like your girlfriend's cooking but you don't want to offend her, some positive reinforcement about how much of a good cook she is might instill more effort when she is cooking next time. This is a bit manipulative, especially in this context, but sometimes instilling the idea, giving higher praise and appreciating that idea when it is not exactly true at the time, may make it true in the future. Shakespeare once wrote, "Assume a virtue, if you have it not." By a moderately extrapolated extension, it follows that assuming a virtue in others may make them want to develop that virtue.

A good leader in business knows how to do the tasks of everyone who reports to them. By achieving this difficult feat you will always have a degree of control when things go wrong, you won't be insecure letting people go for longer holidays, and you will be more able in handling life's curveballs. Because you know the job of each of your employees you also know when they are doing a job well or poorly and therefore you can make better decisions about if the employee is under or over performing your expectations. Better still, replace "expectations" with degrees of appreciation. Remember while many of these core social skills are pivotal for dating and formulating meaningful relationships they can also carry forward in our careers and our individual day-to-day lives.

Tips for Leading:

- Take ballroom dance lessons. Taking dance lessons will make you a better leader because it will force you to think about leading. It will also make your partner more acceptable towards the idea of you leading. Dancing also has a string of other bonuses such as exercise which aligns with the Health Pillar as well as confidence and body posture. Dancing even uses terms like leading, frames and being clear in your intent all of which relate to core social skills. This means you will be automatically more cognitive of the core skills in your everyday life.

- It can be argued that the worst leader is the one that doesn't make a decision. Make a decision, admit when it was the wrong one and learn from it. It's better to keep moving than remain stagnant.

- When a woman asks, "What do you want to do?" she has effectively just given you the lead. Never say, "I don't know, what do you want to do?" This will kill attraction immediately. Decide and go.

- Plan ahead and actually have ideas of things you want to do together. If this is a struggle maybe you are not interested enough in your relationship and you need to figure out why.

- When asking a girlfriend for tips on leading she said, "We really like it when the guy takes control, not in a commanding way but just in a strong leadership way. Wear the pants in the relationship but make sure they are tearaways." So my translation there is take control but don't be forceful or condescending and to obviously invest in tearaways. Wearing tearaways, in this context, could be a metaphor for wearing the pants as a default setting but not developing an ego with leading either. Don't impede your partner if she decides to take initiative.

- Some men might be too strong willed and not listen to what their partner wants. Make sure you acknowledge that their voice is heard. This does not mean stopping what you are doing but it may mean shifting course.

Challenges for Leading:

1. A good leader prepares. This doesn't mean forgoing spontaneity but it means having an idea what you want to do. The challenge is to make a revolving short list of 10 things you want to do so when she gives you that "What do you want to do" line you actually have something you want to do at any given time. Better yet, plan ahead and surprise her with something on your list you want to do that you already set in motion under the full belief that she will go along with it.

2. I challenge you to take a dance lesson with a woman. If you don't have anyone to go with you that just means this is a harder challenge. Dancing, as mentioned, gets you cognitively thinking about leading, inclines the lady to be okay with you leading, improves your body posture, all the while building a whole new skill set that you can use at almost every important social event in your life time.

S2 Non-Essential Social Skills – Tips & Training Wheels

The rest of this Social section is comprised of lesser non-essential core social skills. This means some of the content can be seen as situational or "gamy". These topics are less critical, much more controversial, and overall less important to building the foundation for stronger more meaningful relationships. It follows than that these non-core social section topics and tactics are less pivotal to the overall goal of constant self-improvement relative to the core section.

With that acknowledgement in mind not including them would do you a disservice, as you will encounter many of these themes & topics when you start taking action and meeting potential partners. Many times I felt like quitting because of some of the social walls I ran into as an introverted accountant. However, I then realized just how interesting these topics were, possibly due to "reframing" them. Without these additional tips & training wheels many of you might quit, like I almost did, and give up on yourself which is why I decided to include this content despite some of the controversy around them.

This section can be divided into two parts:

1.) General Tips

2.) Training Wheels

General tips were provided to promote awareness or advice to help make you more confident and able. Unlike training wheel topics, such as "Pick up Lines", these topics, like social awareness & rollercoaster theory you can continue to use while improving yourself. The training wheels topics exist to help ensure you don't let a lack of congruent confidence get the best of you and lead to inaction.

This is a disclaimer. I don't use the words "Training Wheels" lightly. Some of these topics and ideas therein are for the short term. They are not a foundation to build a better you. Do not rely on them and do not make a habit of using them. The training wheel topics are external tools that if relied upon will eventually sap your internal confidence and ability to grow in the long run. Some of these tips will assist you in achieving some of the core critical social skills but it is important to cease using them once they are no longer required. For example, a child's continued use of training wheels when no longer requiring their use for stability only succeeds in undermining their confidence down the road. In dating these tips and training wheels, extended in the long run, will unfortunately serve to provide confidence from something that can be easily taken away. This temporary dependence could essentially make you insecure and limit your intrinsic ability to continue growing. You should view the training wheel topics in this section as things you don't need to do, but can use when you are not confident or when you feel like quitting.

Pick Up Lines

To be clear pick up lines aren't <u>all</u> bad. Remember it's not the words that matter anyway. What matters is how you come across using those words as a medium. Vocal tonality, composure & body posture are all infinitely more important. Pick up lines have their place if only because they automatically convey interest, which means at least you are being forward with your intention. Therefore pick up lines align with the core social skill of being transparently clear in your intent (S1.9). Pick up lines fall directly under the definition of "canned material". Whenever you say the same thing over and over again to different people it means you genuinely don't care about them. You want something from them, probably external validation. Canned material also kills congruency (S1.3) and it means you aren't being authentic to how you are really feeling. This is why pick up lines are associated with being "gamy," but they still have their place. Pick up lines should serve as pool to draw on if you don't feel comfortable meeting people, especially if your brain shuts down due to the body's natural "fight or flight" response catalyzed by social anxiety.

A good pick up line does not draw its "success" from the words in the sentence. Rather, it draws from the context of how you say it and how aware you are of the social stigmas associated with approaching a woman you don't know and conveying that you find her attractive.

For example, let's say you decide to approach a woman with, "Hey, You're a 9 and I'm the 1 you need." This, by itself, generally does not come off as flattery. A 9 means you are directly ranking her against other women which can be easily translated to objectifying her. Worse, if you come off as cocky when you say that line or as if you were trying to get a reaction it is likely to impart arrogance or egotism. Chances are you may have also just interrupted someone in the middle of something.

Finally it likely comes off as a line you have probably used before. However, just by adding some sort of wink, grin, body rock and or casual body/facial expression, you convey that you know the line is cheesy and that she is likely busy, is actually the only way you are likely to extract any positive reaction. The fact that you are cognitively aware it is a cheesy thing to say but went ahead and said it anyway relays a sense of confidence and provides value because you are illustrating that she is worth putting yourself in a potentially vulnerable setting. Additionally, the fact that you aren't after anything from her except for maybe a smile means that the odds are much greater that you will get some type of positive feedback.

A woman who is used to men approaching her may test your "pick up line" by challenging it. "Is that the best you've got?" At which point you'd better have an answer as this is a pretty standard reaction to any pick up line. However, these "challenges" are not a flat out rejection. A lady knows when you approach with a cheesy pick up line that it means you are interested in her as pickup lines are always clear in their intent. A rejection would be ignoring you, saying "no", or that she's not interested, or for that matter any physical body positioning that says "No". I will talk about some of the common challenges you are likely to run across and how to handle them in the next section under Handling Tests.

Now you are probably going to ask, "What is the best pick up line?"

The "best" pick up line is a very complicated process:

1.) Walk directly to her and attempt to make eye contact.

2.) Introduce yourself and tell her what made you decide to introduce yourself.

3.) When carrying out step 2 customize when you introduce yourself to how you are feeling at that time.

This is the best pick up line as it is congruent, clear in your intent, simple yet not canned or fake, genuine, confident and makes yourself vulnerable. It is also dynamic which means it is always changing, thus forcing you to be more actively engaged instead of just reciting lines. The trick is to not personalize any positive or negative reaction. You don't need her validation and you know she isn't rejecting you because she hasn't had the opportunity to really know who you are. Making it personal introduces an ego and therefore needs to be avoided at all costs.

I know the "best pick up line" is a bit bold, brave and not for everyone when you're not comfortable with yourself or find yourself situationally down in the self-confidence department. Therefore, listed below are some pick up lines I have used personally when I too also felt a little unconfident. Most of these are cheesy and I embody them that way but most importantly I have fun saying them to people. These are all tailored for certain situations.

- "Do you have a twin?" (No) "Oh! Then you must be the most beautiful girl in the world." This is a pretty standard pick up line. It accomplishes its primary function which is to express intent. It also forces her to answer which is a double edged sword. It means you need her to react to you at a time where she may not know yet if she wants to. Therefore, it takes value but then gives it back again in the form of a compliment. This is a cheesy pick up line and consequently you should convey it in a knowingly cheesy way.

- "Your shirt looks nice, what's it made out of? [Brief Pause, Don't wait for a reply] "Girlfriend material?" [Say with the tonality like it was a question]. "Hmm let me see the tag to make sure" [Pause while actively fake checking the tag; don't actually touch her] "Like I thought." [Pause] "Made in heaven." This is over the top cheesy. It generally works well if the woman is semi used to men approaching her. She obviously needs to know that you don't actually care what her shirt is made out of and that you are interested in her. Starting off with complimenting her shirt means you are likely to be able to finish the routine because it's light, harmless and will most likely make her smile right off the bat.

- "Hey! Are you drunk? (Yes or No) [Don't react to what the response is] "Okay I'll come back later then." This is obviously very situational. I personally use it because I find it hilarious especially when she says yes because then she is usually really confused. Obviously only use in clubs. This isn't a real pick up line since you are almost ensuring "defeat" at the beginning but it sets the seeds for something when you see her again later that night. Make sure you say it in a way that she knows that you don't actually want her drunk or else she might think you're a creep. Given this is a 10 second interaction with you actively ejecting yourself it requires good use of sub-communication.

- "My friends bet me I wouldn't talk to the most beautifully daunting girl in the room. Want to buy a drink with their money?" This is a standard pick up line. It provides value to her but diminishes yours because you are in effect bribing her time with a drink. This could translate into you not thinking you offer enough value just by being yourself. This line does give the lady the avenue of "I just wanted a free drink" if you guys quickly find out you don't have any chemistry. It follows then that this is a less pressured social interaction.

Generally the only time I used this line is if I wanted people other than her to see me socializing with someone for "Social Proof." Social Proof and its implications will be mentioned later.

- "Hey! What would you say to me to get my attention, because I can't come up with anything for you right now?" Be careful with this line because it does take value from her. You are directly asking her for something creative on the spot. This line is only used when you actually can't think of anything to say and she is giving you clear signs of interest with her body language (i.e. eye contact, preening and body movements). It follows then that any hesitation on your part might ruin it. This line really needs to be in the moment and really it is contingent on her making the first move with body language.

- "You look fabulous! [Pause] For your age." This is best used on women who are noticeably fairly young (21-30) and should only be used on women that are older than you if they appear fun and cheerful. Obviously a lady could be insecure about her age especially if she is older, so make sure to always say this in a fun and happy-go-lucky way regardless of what their actual age appears. This line also introduces the **rollercoaster theory** where you compliment her and then abruptly take the compliment away creating a type of rollercoaster of emotion. This "give and take" mentality is extremely effective at creating excitement and showing that you aren't the typical boring predictable guy that she's accustomed to. That being said, if she isn't accustomed to men conveying interest in her then you don't really need to utilize any type of rollercoaster tactics. Just remember to always leave her happier than when she was before you started the conversation.

- "Do you know how I got these guns?" [Point to biceps] "Saving (something small/cute) from (something dangerous)." This is another over the top pick up line. It's hilarious and carefree, especially if you don't actually have big arms, because then it also indicates that you don't take yourself so seriously and likely aren't egotistical, arrogant or insecure. This isn't a true pick up line since you would need to convey your intention with your body language. Unlike the other pick up lines you are talking about yourself instead of talking about her, consequentially drawing the attention to yourself, and letting her handle that sentence any way she wants to. If she ever replies "I guess the (something cute noun) needs more help" {and flex's too} then you may have just found your life partner!

As a caveat, before you decide to go the pick up line route, always be smiling. To be fair, you should already always be smiling when meeting someone if you've mastered that part of the core social section under the Law of State Transference (S1.5).

Make sure not to spam the woman with pick up lines one after the other. The pick up line is just a tool used when you feel you need to show your interest. Saying pick up line after pick up line to the same person means you are being "gamy" and not really giving her a chance to get to know you. You are effectively being a stand-up comedian. That being said, it's better to be funny than to get a negative reaction but again that depends on what your intention is.

The common trend with these pickup lines is that they are generally light and carefree. My favorites are cheesy lines because society already views pickup lines as cheesy. Therefore use your social acuity and embrace the cheesiness society expects, making sure you illustrate that you know it's cheesy with your sub-communication along the way.

Canned material ultimately, as already mentioned, is not the default way to go. Canned material is prepared ahead of time, which means it is judged much more harshly, and it should be. Recall improv and "in the moment" action will always have the lower bar for judgement and it is generally much more respected than pick up lines. In closing, don't use canned material if it can be avoided, but if you need a temporary boost of confidence so that you don't freeze up from inaction don't hesitate to pull one or two out. Use them sparingly and at your discretion.

How to Persevere Through "Tests"

A "test" is when a woman challenges you in any way. A test is not a "No". A "No" is a "No". If you say something and then she replies anything along the lines of, "is that it?" This really is a challenge. She has just given you an opportunity to convey value. Ladies want to know who exactly it is that they are talking to so they want to test you to see if you are who you are coming across as. She wants to know are you really that "cool guy" or just another pretender? These tests are actually good, or at least frame them in that way when they happen. And they will happen. Most women don't just go up to a random "loser" and say, "Look at yourself, you're pathetic, is that all you got?" Frame any test she gives you as a social cue that she wants to get to know you better.

So how do you pass these tests?

Mostly with indifference. Don't try to think logically or defend yourself. You don't need cocky, witty answers but cocky witty answers can work. View the test as a frame the lady is trying to impose on the interaction. Visualize that she is trying to put you into a pre-set "cookie cutter" interaction that she already knows. Responding quickly (think free word association) and brushing them off is the best way to beat a "test". For example, the standard, "Hey, I'm not a photographer, but I can picture me and you together" is challenged with "Is that all you got?" Your response could be "I've got more but nothing that will do a woman as pretty as you justice." Obviously this is cocky, but it will work in this situation because it is playful and you obviously came across as "gamy" which is why she tested you. Therefore you embrace her frame but so abruptly that it implies you were expecting it and didn't care that she called you on your pick up line.

Remember she wants you to pass these tests, so don't clam up or get defensive. She wouldn't test you if she didn't hope that you would pass. A no is a no, not a test, so don't pursue a no. She's rooting for you but she wants to see who you really are.

Openers

Openers are the first things you do or say when you initially meet someone. Pick up lines are direct openers, meaning they directly convey "Hey, I am attracted to you." However, openers don't have to be direct, which means they are less likely to be viewed as "gamy" but they also are less likely to be congruent with your intention. These less direct openers can be useful for building social proof, momentum & confidence. Most indirect traditional openers are framed as a question which means the lady has to reply. Such as, "Who do you think cheats more, men or women?" Attempting to make a women that doesn't know you reply to something is taking away from her. This is why you should always advocate being direct above any type of indirect opener. Congruent in the moment sincere appreciation **is greater than** cheesy canned material pick up line **is greater than** indirect opener. And I say that as an introverted accountant from Canada who you think would favor being indirect.

Openers do put less pressure on the woman at the onset of the interaction. However, this perk is partially offset as you run the risk of being put into the "friend zone" because she doesn't know what your intentions are. Are you just trying to be social and friendly? Did you really want to know "if you look like a drug dealer?" just to facilitate conversation. Or are you trying to tell her you are attracted to her but don't know how. She won't know unless you know. What if she logically pins it wrong and thinks you are just being friendly when you wanted a potential date? That's on you, not her. And it's because you weren't confident enough in your ability just to say, "Hey, I don't normally do this but you seem really nice and I would have regretted not at least saying hi to you!"

Despite the above slam on indirect openers and canned material in general, the following are some basic openers you could use to get your mouth talking and gather some momentum to alleviate some social anxiety.

- "Who do you think cheats more, Men or Women?" This creates a base sexual topic to open on. It is a bit personal but it does promote engagement. Useful in groups at a bar or club. A perk with this opener is you could readily link to convey intention contingent on where you are planning to go with the question.

- Do you think this <point at whatever you are wearing> is too (adjective)?" This works best when you genuinely think whatever you are wearing could be seen as "too" much of whatever you think it is. Example: if I were to wear short shorts then I might say, "Do you think these <point to shorts> are too revealing? The best openers should be seen as genuine and in the moment. However, since they are really pre-planned it can be manipulative. Please note: Manipulation is a zero-sum paradigm trait, not a value adding one. Since indirect openers take value on the onset you have to ensure you add a compensating amount of value after the opener. Make sure her answering your question is worth her while.

- Situational Openers – These openers are simply turning to someone immediately when something happens and making an observation about it. These are in the moment and are therefore genuine and authentic. The shortfall is you can't make things happen and lingering around someone you are interested in waiting for something around them to happen is likely to be seen as creepy. Situational openers are least likely to be seen as conveying any type of interest. Is your intention to make conversation or find a potential life partner? Situational openers are best used just to get you to start speaking and taking action from an in the moment mindset.

Just like with pick up lines, the amount of openers are endless. I only put in a few examples as I feel indirect openers embody less Core Social Skills and leave more maneuverability for manipulation. Openers are best used in a group setting to start the flow of conversation and include everyone. For example, say there is a group of 4 attractive ladies and you are really taken with one of them. It is far easier to open with, "Who do you think cheats more, Men or Women?" than it is to walk right into their group and say, "I think you are really pretty and I wanted to say hi. Did you want to dance?" Either can work but obviously if she says "no" to dancing in front of all her friends then you or even her could feel shamed or embarrassed. If you've mastered those Core Social Skills and don't have an ego it shouldn't bother you that she said "no". You shouldn't feel embarrassed because I bet the next lady you ask will say yes assuming you remain composed. You will stand out just for putting yourself daringly out there like that. Later on when you start dancing with another girl having fun and smiling, some part of the initial women's brain will probably wish she said yes. Remember your intention is always trying to find "the one", not start a survey on "what gender society think cheats more."

It is in everyone's best interest to be as transparent as possible and not give in to what's easier. The more vulnerable society sees you making yourself the more likely the woman will want to say yes. A lady doesn't want to be seen as the "bad guy". While a "no" may hurt your ego I highly doubt her friends would laugh unless they associate with negativity or have an unhealthy association of their self-worth stemming from social validation. The act of walking up to a woman in front of her friends, with the sheer belief she will say "yes" to your request to a dance, will make it extremely probable that she will want to accept. The only reason I decided to have any section at all on indirect openers are because they do build social proof and momentum (S1.6). However they leave room for being un-genuine & manipulative when they are pre-planned. Furthermore these indirect openers are actively against being clear in your intent (S1.9). This leads to mixed messages & misunderstandings and don't exactly set the framework to start a potential relationship on the right path. The more indirect you are the more likely you are to find yourself "friend-zoned". Therefore if you have a theme of being friend-zoned then it is likely you struggle with conveying intent. Remember if you mastered the Core Social Skills then confidence will come from within. It doesn't matter if there is one acquaintance with the woman you like, or 8 of her friends, you should act with the same confidence. Situational confidence is not true confidence. Just be aware that women do judge each other and this fear of being judged can alter her decision. Tailor accordingly. Typically no woman will be shamed by her peers for saying "yes" or "no" to a dance request with a man who seems to know what he is about.

Roller Coaster Theory and Negatives/Negs:

Roller coaster theory, as briefly touched upon during the pick up lines section, is spiking her emotions in an up and down pattern with an overall trend up. It means complimenting her, bringing her up and then debasing the pedestal you created, but not so much that she is feeling worse off than she did initially. Most women who are fairly attractive will enjoy this pattern on a subconscious level. It makes you unpredictable which means you aren't just another typical guy. It doesn't have to be happy/sad. It can simply be exciting, boring, exciting. If you are constantly Mr. Nice guy or constantly negative than you are not engaging. If a woman thinks you are boring then your conversation is too basic and not stimulating engagement. If the conversation feels boring to you then it follows that it's probably boring to her. Boredom in this context originates from being guarded and afraid to express yourself. The fear of genuinely expressing yourself actually makes the interaction more likely to fail. It is a self-fulfilling prophecy. Chances are if you are found to be "boring" you are really just putting on a front to guard yourself from her judgement. Even if you identity with the trait of "being boring" you still do have passions and interests. If you don't, then what is driving you to wake up in the morning? It is much more likely you are afraid to express yourself in your entirety and it's sabotaging your chances of finding a good life partner.

The most risk free way to do any type of polarizing activity is simply alternate between being silly and being serious. Being serious utilizes the more typical questions like: who she is, what she does for a living, who she is with, has she always lived in this city, etc. The serious conversation is to get to know her on a logical level. The silly topics are not as uniform and should be composed of things you want to talk about that you find interesting. It can be over the top if that's what you are feeling, be congruent with your mood. You just approached a random woman you are attracted to so you are already going to be fairly engaged and excited. Therefore the Law of State Transference (S1.5) will make her want to be engaged in what you are saying as well. Talking seriously continually or asking too many questions in a row is likely to leave her disengaged or adversely make her feel like she is at an interview. On the other hand, saying too many silly things might make you seem not exactly with it. The trick is to balance and calibrate how you feel with how the overall interaction is going.

A true "Rollercoaster" is mixing compliments in with "Negs". A neg is a backhanded compliment. A negs main purpose should be used just to surprise her as most guys won't be comfortable ever teasing with a neg. A neg may also serve to make the woman feel that she has to prove herself in some way. Never neg a woman that doesn't need it. That is, don't tease a woman that can't take being teased. This is akin to how a women won't test a man who she thinks can't handle a test. As an example why not use former US president Calvin Coolidge. Due to the popularity of certain books it is now common knowledge that Mr. Coolidge was quite quiet. One morning Mr. Coolidge said to his secretary "That's a pretty dress you are wearing this morning, and you are a very attractive young woman." It was so unusual that the secretary blushed in confusion. Then Coolidge said, "Now, don't get stuck up. I just said that to make you feel good. From now on, I wish you would be more careful with your punctuation." Obviously the former president was not hitting on his secretary, but the example stands. With rollercoaster theory it is generally best to start with the positive comment/topic before the negative. As Dale Carnegie mentions, "It is always easier to listen to relatively less pleasant things after we have heard some admiration for our good points". Put the appreciation first before you decide to neg. If you find yourself in a situation in approaching a lady who society has constantly reinforced to her that she is attractive than make sure you say your neg in close <u>proximity</u> to your appreciation. Because she is constantly being appreciated she will not respond to your appreciation but she will respond to your neg. The more attractive the woman the closer the proximity should be between the compliment and the neg. This is because until that neg is said you are just the fifteenth man that day that decided to interrupt her. Remember a neg isn't mean, it's playful. If she seems haughty, attractive and full of herself with confidence than try it out. Remember to always tease from a friendly carefree place and **not** a mean & negative "give me a reaction" now place.

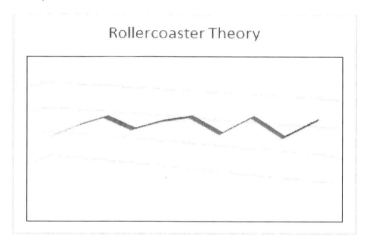

Rollercoaster Theory

Some typical negs are:

- "I wish I could be as confident as you and dress like that."

- "Wow, you look fit, that bicep is borderline intimidating."

- "I like you. You have the boldness of a much younger woman."

- "You are so cute but that laugh though."

Merging Groups of People:

Introducing one group of people you just met into another group you just met is a sure way to create excitement. Merging groups is important as it makes you automatically "interesting" and adds value due to the fact you have everyone out of their comfort zone and meeting new people. Everyone will automatically be engaged and their eyes will light up merely because they aren't used to this behavior. Merging groups is said to be more advanced and it is because you have to know with body language which groups want to have fun and meet new friends etc.... You have to believe firmly inside that everyone will be better off by meeting each other.

So why does this work for finding a potential life partner?

1.) First it conveys a fun social attitude. You are automatically the leader of the interaction because everyone knows you the most so they will likely, initially, have their attention on you since you are the bridging conduit between them. As a bonus you get to revel as the literal causation of this excited state.

2.) Social proof – It means you have "friends" to the next group. They don't know you barely know the people you introduced them to. Having "friends" automatically makes you less creepy to anyone you decide to meet. It means you are less likely to be viewed as awkward or "weird". This is especially true at a club venue where the social norm is to always have friends inside the venue with you.

3.) Momentum – Meeting multiple people in a short time frame builds a magnitude of momentum. Suddenly you will subconsciously start viewing the venue as a friendly place, surrounded by people who want to get to know this guy who seemingly knows everyone in the bar.

4.) Preselection – A woman is more likely to view you as a potential life partner if other women are also attracted to you. It validates their decision that you might be a "good catch" if other women think that too. This is done internally and is not cognitively processed.

Merging a group inevitably appoints yourself as the temporary leader of the merged group and interestingly enough makes it so any emotion you decide to express is amplified. Merging groups is not for everyone and it can sacrifice being direct or romantic. That being said, if you want to challenge and improve your social ability and have the best random evenings that make the most meaningful long term memories... then learn to merge groups. It is more chaotic and less linear, but makes you feel really good for doing things most people aren't comfortable doing. I have actually merged groups of people who became lifelong friends and still visit each other over great distances and my own intention at that time was just to meet an attractive woman in another group. I personally find it humorous as approximately 100% of the time, at least initially, the other group will assume I am good friends with the people whom I just introduced them to. Make sure you ask the group, "how they all know each other," as this is a great way to open the door for social networking whilst getting to know the group dynamics and hopefully provide insight about your potential significant other within the natural context of her friends.

Oddly enough merging groups can be used in a way to leave a women with a good impression. If the conversation starts dying and your personalities were a bit at ends you could simply go and introduce her to a group. That way it would add one little bit of value to her while you could leave and always come back in later to say hi or use that group as social proof for fun. Social networking is critically important for long term financial success so why not start practicing now. You would be surprised how even after just one merged group the "stereotypical introverted accountant" looks like he knows everybody at the venue.

Beware in attempting to merge a group with a group that is giving off "our group wants to be alone" body language. An example would be a group that is closed off in a corner disengaged with everyone but themselves. The sun you bring with you can quickly be eaten by a group enforced black hole.

Ultimately, merging groups is not that important in the overall scheme of finding a significant other but you could use this exercise to improve your social networking ability in a relatively low risk environment. This way you are prepared and can more capably handle important events down the road. What better place to learn these social skills then practicing them now with real people in less nerve wracking scenarios?

Appreciation vs. Flattery

Do things for the right reasons. Just because you went up to a stranger and mentioned she was pretty doesn't mean she owes you anything. Dale Carnegie in "How to Win Friends and Influence People" actually writes this point on Appreciation vs. Flattery extremely well:

"The difference between appreciation and flattery? That is simple. One is sincere and the other insincere. One comes from the heart out; the other from the teeth out. One is unselfish; the other selfish. One is universally admired; the other universally condemned."

While flattery is not "universally condemned" anymore, remember to be sincere when you compliment your potential life partner. If you walk up and say, "I like your dress," like the 100 guys before you and don't mean it... then it is gamy. If you do mean it, it could be attractive. If she challenges you with "what do you like about it?" then she is trying to see if you actually appreciate it or if you are just trying to hook up with her like the people before you.

Appreciation gives value whereas flattery is generally associated with wanting something in return. A tip here is simply to remember the difference and utilize the word "appreciation" in your day to day life. This small tip of using appreciation in your jargon will literally make people around you feel like you genuinely do appreciate them. When a woman says she wants appreciation it means she wants genuine compliments and acknowledgment. This is why when she tells you to "appreciate her more" and then you immediately compliment her she likely still won't be content. This is because the forced timing of the compliment is indicative of flattery, not sincere appreciation. Talk is cheap but genuine emotions are invaluable.

Going out Alone vs. Enlisting A Wingman:

There are pros and cons of going out alone vs. having a good friend or group of friends to go out with. For the purposes of self-development it is suggested to be able and confident enough to go out alone.

When you go out for the first time alone to a venue to perhaps meet someone you are attracted to, it is surprisingly intimidating. Why can one easily buy food at a store for themselves alone but feel apprehensive going in solo to a lounge, bar or club? The main reason here is social conditioning. People typically always go to lounges, bars and clubs with other people. You might think you can go to that club alone but waiting in that long line outside the venue for the first time, I guarantee you will feel like everyone is judging you, even the glorified doorman. You have to remember no one actually knows you are alone, for all they know your friends could be inside. They will only pick up that you are alone if you stand alone by yourself inside the venue for a long period of time. Therefore, it's likely this internal torment is just in your head. No one cares that you went out alone as much as you do. And you only care that much because society ingrained it into you that you need someone to go out with. Going out alone makes you self-reliant and makes it so you are more cognitively aware of the emotions you alone are bringing into your conversations with women. If you think going out alone is weird you will give off weird/uncertain emotional vibes to the lady which means she won't be able to know what you are about. This is commonly labeled as being creepy. Going out alone makes you accountable to yourself.

So what does a wingman provide?

A wingman does have its merits. First, it's more socially acceptable, gives easy social proof (so you don't appear aloof) and also brings a degree of competition, fun and moral support.

To tie into self-development for the purposes of dating, if you decide to use a wingman, use that wingman like something you don't want to use. The ideal wingman, is someone you go inside the venue with and never see again until the next time you go out. Too many people hang out with their wingman all night and don't take action to meet a potential significant other. Or worse behave differently around their wingman than how they are in real life. Kind of like "Grease" with John Travolta and Oliva Newton-John. Don't pull a "Danny Zuko" and change identities based on who is around you. Don't be a chameleon. Be yourself. Be strong. Be congruent. How can a woman date you for the long run if you have an identity that changes based on who is around you. She will never really know who you are and for that matter you probably won't either.

In the long run it is better to go out alone, at least for the purpose of improving oneself. It makes you accountable for yourself and you won't be able to rely on anyone except for yourself. A wingman is effectually a crutch. You shouldn't need anyone, even if it's a willing friend. While a wingman can bring an array of social proof and motivation to keep going when people reject you it is better to learn how to pull that motivation from within. An unhealthy reliance on a wingman can stagnant your self-development "gains" and compromise your congruence.

Tips for going out alone:

- Don't drink. Not one. Not ever. This way you can circumvent danger, drive yourself to and from the venue, and keep your wits about you all while saving your liver and wallet, which just so happen to be the other two Pillars of this book.

- Don't appear alone. Talk to people. Relate and establish meaningful relations with strangers.

- The first few times you go out you alone you will be nervous. Recall what your intention is and lower the bar for success so you don't beat yourself up too much. Instead of trying to find a life partner, set your intention for the night to just saying "hi" to five women you are attracted to. Only you can regulate your emotions and know what you are capable of/comfortable with at any one time. No one else knows your emotions and capabilities better than you.

- Own up to being alone when someone asks where your friends are. A lady will ask where your friends are as a conversation builder or as a test if she thinks you are alone. Odds are at least ~60-70% won't believe you anyway if you answer truthfully because they can't fathom that reality due to how socially conditioned we all are about going out alone. Owning up to this off the bat however makes you different and interesting. Just make sure you aren't weird or dodgy about being out alone. If she asks why, make sure you aren't defensive as she isn't calling you "weird". You need to frame that going out alone is for self-development, building confidence in yourself and hopefully meeting the right girl along the way. Hell, you could even say that to her if you truly believed it.

Social Anxiety:

Everyone has social anxiety. Social anxiety will never go away. Being aware of social anxiety, unlike being aware of an ego, doesn't alleviate it. Instead, it makes it worse. Social anxiety stifles you, makes you afraid to express your true self in fear of social judgement, and therein inhibits your ability to be congruent, genuine and vulnerable to your potential life partner.

The best thing you can do with social anxiety is challenge it. By challenging social anxiety, I mean to embrace it. Once you accept that it is okay to be afraid of approaching a stranger then at least you are on even ground to combat it. That way you acknowledge why you talk fast or start sweating when you finally build up the courage to speak to a women who has been approached multiple times a week with a line that she has probably heard a million times before. Now that you have accepted social anxiety, instead of being defensive towards it, the next step to beat social anxiety is to take action. Once you have a few conversations where you manage to walk away with all body parts intact your body will become temporarily numb to any previous socially conditioned fears. I say temporarily as social anxiety always edges its way back into your body over time through natural societal conditioning.

Why do you feel anxious?

Ask yourself why you are scared of approaching this really attractive women who spent thirty minutes painting her face and one hour on her hair? On a subconscious level, people will want some degree of social validation for their time and effort in making themselves look stunning and won't say no to a genuine compliment. Frame it as a win/win. You want her to be better off by having met you, even if it is just for a few minutes. Make sure you value yourself. I mean, you read self-help books and are constantly striving to be the best version of yourself so you have odds of being a better catch than the average guy out there right? SO do her a favor and let her know what you are about!

Understandably, social anxiety intensity from cold approaching strangers is exponentially higher than from online dating. I found, and you probably will to, that pre-planned dates via online are an easy way to reduce or completely eliminate social anxiety. This is largely because there is now a 0% chance that you "rudely" interrupted a women while she was busy doing something else. That being said, you may still be anxious for your first few online dates just because you aren't used to the social scenario. In my experience, unlike the social anxiety from cold approach, the social anxiety from online dating went away completely and never came back. This is largely because the lady has agreed to meet you already. Online dating allows you to lay to rest the worry that she might not be interested in you. She would not have agreed to meet you if she wasn't interested.

You won't die by approaching a woman. As William Shakespeare once wrote in Julius Caesar, "A coward dies a thousand times before his death, but the valiant taste of death but once." Each time you don't summon the courage to voice your admiration for a potential significant other you die a little bit inside. Instead of focusing on the repercussion of not approaching, i.e. denying yourself what you truly want, you should be focused on the potential reward. The reward being a truly loving, long-lasting relationship. Always focus on the positive outcome.

No matter how any interaction goes, every time you "escape unscathed" should be framed as another reference you can later draw on. This reference makes the future you more resolute and resilient. Beating social anxiety is important as the woman wants to meet the real you. Not the anxious you. Not the you who is more worried about the conversation and how the date goes in its entirety, than from actually trying to express who you really are.

In conclusion, there is no way around social anxiety. Online dating helps relieve most of social anxiety's pressure. Embracing social anxiety, accepting it and then taking constant action against it is the only way to conquer your social anxiety fears and even then your victory will be temporary in nature.

Peacocking:

Peacocking, as defined by Urban dictionary is, "dressing for attention, just like how Peacock's use their feathers to attract a mate."

While I am not saying paint your nails black and glue peacock feathers to your hat, I am suggesting to at least wear one piece of attire or accessory that stands out. The piece that you decide to "display" should be something the woman would notice and comment on if she decided to talk to you. While guys are commonly the ones who should make the first move to display attraction and open themselves up to some degree of vulnerability, a women may want to introduce herself to you as well. An easy way to make sure the lady has an avenue to do that is to have something visual she can easily comment on.

How subtle vs. ridiculous you take peacocking is up to how congruent the piece in question ties in with your personality. If you are a shy guy it's not recommended to run around a club in a tall purple hat and pimp jacket. That screams for attention which you may not be able to handle congruently. A superhero shirt at one point would have been peacocking but nowadays most superhero shirts are mainstream. Remember you want to be subtle but also give her something to comment on that's unique to your personality or just to you. But if you can list all the Avengers go ahead and rock that Avenger shirt!

As mentioned the type of accessory doesn't matter. What matters most is to make sure the item you decide to showcase aligns with your personality, or quite frankly it would make you a bit of a poser. Even a tacky old Mickey Mouse watch could suffice if it means something to you. Any item that is unique and has important value to you would be more than enough to fulfill the criteria of "peacocking."

Proper Grooming

As a deviation from peacocking make sure you take care of your grooming image and sustain proper hygiene. This is a no brainer, but unfortunately many guys decide not to use their brains. As will be talked about in the health section, visually showing you take care of your health is a tangible indicator that you likely value yourself and therein have a high sense of self-esteem. Valuing yourself means it is likely women will value you as well. Failure to illustrate that you value yourself shows that you don't think much of yourself so why should a stranger. Actions will always speak louder than words. Comb that hair, brush your teeth, take a shower, clean those nails and wash your hands after using the bathroom! One should err on the side of not wearing clothes that have rips in them but if it's congruent with your identity go for it. Great grooming and keeping yourself clean shows that you have respect for yourself and for everyone else you come into contact with throughout the day. What easier way to show you believe in yourself than by simply taking pride in your appearance. A woman you are interested in can make up her mind about you before you even open your mouth so don't make it harder on yourself by wearing something unbecoming if it can be avoided.

Dealing With Rejection

Accept rejection. Your intent is not to avoid rejection; recall the Core Social Skill of being clear in your intent. Your true intent, rather, is to express that you are attracted to someone who you think has the potential to be a good life partner.

She doesn't know anything about you. Just like you don't really know anything about her, at least that's not surface shallow. She does not know you, so she can't reject you. That being said, when you approach someone and she blows you off, allow it to happen. It is normal for this to happen. Don't have an ego about it. People have lives and interests of their own. Everyone isn't compatible with just anyone so don't expect everyone to be compatible with you.

So how should you view rejection when it happens?

Don't personalize it. Reframe rejection as a good thing. You went up, conveyed your intention, and hopefully made her smile or laugh or even made her evening. It is out of your control if she wasn't attracted to you or had a boyfriend or was busy, etc. Rejection makes you stronger because it teaches you how to deal with failure and how to be outcome independent. Imagine you are a tree, self-improvement makes you taller and broader but dealing with failure and temporary setbacks allow your roots to dig deeper which creates the foundation for you to grow even taller. Now imagine that tree is a spoiled kid who never had to work for anything but had "everything". What if he lost "everything"? Do you think he would be capable enough to build back that bank account, sports car and mansion his parents originally gave to him? What if you never really understood what an ego was? How would this kid handle someone saying "no" to him? Would he know how to deal with it? Or would he throw an immature tantrum and lash out at everyone around him in an effort to preserve his ego? In a windstorm that man-child would fall over and never be able to pick himself up. Don't be an entitled man-child. Allow for rejection, don't fear it and definitely don't personalize it. Reframe it as a good thing and you'll keep that internal upward spiral going regardless of reactions from anyone around you.

Social Acuity – Macro Fads and Trends

Be aware of the world around you. Know the social fads and trends. This doesn't mean react or go with these social tendencies but be aware of them. If the social fad goes with your identity then make sure to embrace it when you can. If the social fad goes against your identity make sure you know you are not in the majority. For example, this book is written in a way to try to make a guy going up to a women he likes not as socially condemning as it currently is. Guy's, when approaching a girl he likes, with the intention of conveying interest can get pegged as "pick up artist" all too nonchalantly. Society constantly tells a man to "man up", and when he does he gets condemned for it by society when it works and shamed by his fellow man and himself when he gets rejected. By extension, I know just in the act of writing this book that it could also be condemned, as some of the content is "gamy," and I know there will be some similarities with pick up artists especially in attracting a woman in the short-term and with my multiple references to Owen Cook from RSD.

The following three paragraphs are a bit of a tangent that I felt compelled to insert here despite my editor's recommendations. In a proactive attempt to circumvent this potential social condemnation of "promoting gamy tactics", I tailored the content to utilize more socially acceptable words and phrases. That being said even with those words and phrases it would be for not because this book would still go against the grain, as it could be put in the context of going against extreme feminism. For the record this book is not against feminism at all. Everyone should be equal. It is just that the social power behind feminism is so strong that I am aware how lightly I have to tread around certain concepts. Instead of attacking feminism, which for the record (again) the actual idea of feminism I am not at all against, my book leverages off of other social trends like self-improvement and the staggering high divorce statistic (which I truly believe is a hard fact that society is wrong when it comes to building loving relationships). While utilizing this book itself as an example is more than a little unorthodox and admittedly slightly digressive to the overall book message, I want you to take away that when you have to go against society its best to bring in other social concepts to back you up.

For example:

Someone might think this book is "anti-feminist" therefore I must pin equally strong social trends against this view so that the points I make will invoke thought instead of instant rejection. In the case of this book I used the up swinging social self-improvement trend, paired with well-known and documented current social fact weakness (i.e. high divorce rate) and finally tailored it with the intention of a long term relationship.

Luckily you are not writing a book that could be interpreted as going against a current up swinging social trend. The long winded point of this tangent is that you need to **be aware** when what you are saying could be unpopular, especially in a public setting.

Alright so what should I do if I am indifferent towards a social trend?

If you are neutral with a social trend then don't be afraid to try it temporarily, if only to form an opinion. If you never grew a lumberjack beard yet in 2016 or a man bun... it is currently socially acceptable to try. Social fads are an easy way for someone to get a point of reference from you. Conversations on dates typically do dance around social trends, so the more opinions (good or bad) and experiences you have with them, the easier the woman you are attracted to can become comfortable around you.

If your identity aligns with a social trend make sure you let the world know. Embrace it. Leverage off it. Embracing a social trend makes it easy to be remembered because the person will subconsciously link you to a social trend they already know. Embracing or contrasting with a stereotype or established social trend will let people identify who you are faster. Embracing something your potential significant other is likely to agree with also creates an easier, positive way, to build some bridges of commonality. There is an Ancient Chinese Proverb that states: "He who treads softly goes far". If the woman is starting to identify with you because of your agreement on some macro social trends or fads it's much easier to get her to start accepting other things about yourself that may have been more up to chance. This is called the "**Socratic method**" and is based on getting a yes, yes response. Basically, use your knowledge of social trends to bridge a positive "yes" response. This seemingly small thing helps get both of you moving in an affirmative direction. This is a low risk way to start the "things seem to be going well" mentality.

Surprisingly, in the act of expressing yourself, people seem to want to distinguish themselves by not conforming to social fads. This can go to the extent of changing ones identity temporarily just to go against that social norm...that is until the social norm is no longer popular. While it is good to stand out in the short term for contrast, which lets her more quickly determine your identity, it is not good for a long term relationship since you are actually lying to yourself and her about who you are. Going against a social trend or fad just to spite it because it is popular could uncover some underlying stratagem of attempting to get a sense of your own importance by antagonizing others. This is gamy and at its best only helps you in the short run. Even then this potential short term benefit is situational because you are in fact likely conflicting against her interests which she knows are mainstream.

In closing, to improve your social acuity simply know what's "hot" & what's "not". Don't ignore those common trending topics on your Facebook or Twitter feeds. Embrace the social trends that go with your identity and conversely, circumvent the ones that don't. Don't compromise your identity to conform or contrast just for the sake of going along or contrasting the social camaraderie. Take action on any trends or fads that you happen to be neutral with; it is always worth your while to form an opinion if only to facilitate easy conversation with people in your day to day life. This easy, light hearted, some would argue "filler" conversation, can and does help build momentum which is a Core Social Skill (S1.6).

Social Empathy – Emotional Intelligence & Calibration

As an extension of the social macro trends you also need to be aware of how the women you are interested in is feeling at a micro level. Not to react to how they are feeling but instead to identify how they are feeling and lead much more effectively. Empathy is the ability to understand and share the feelings of another which is a critical trait of a great leader; a core competency (S1.10).

Social calibration is the most effective way to consciously effect social empathy. This social calibration is most important when first getting to know your potential significant other. If you are already in a relationship chances are you and your significant will already be socially calibrated to each other.

Curiously, social calibration starts from within, not from the social interaction itself. Are you aware of how people view you and how you view yourself? What emotional energy are you putting out when you go up and say hi to that woman you are crazy about? Are you self-fulfilled or do you need something from the interaction? This self-awareness is what comes across when you introduce yourself to an individual. It combines Congruency (S1.3) and the Law of State Transference (S1.5). Being aware of this bench mark base setting and asking yourself these questions helps you know how you are coming across to the women you are interested in before you even open your mouth.

The next step is the actual calibration. Calibrate yourself and the things you are likely to say, so you don't appear socially outlandish or out to lunch. This is being aware of how you are effecting the women you like. Do they want to talk to you? Are they conveying interest back towards you? If the woman turns out to be shy perhaps you should tone down the forwardness? Don't change yourself but dial into how she is feeling. If she shows discomfort at being the center of attention, don't talk so loud or be as expressive. You should be figuring out what type of topics she is open to at the time and which ones are taboo. What topics cause her eyes light up on and which ones does she brush aside? All women are unique so don't ignore the social cues they are giving you. Calibrating yourself is not changing who you are. You are just fine tuning yourself so as to assist in making sure she is comfortable in her being herself to you.

An additional level of social calibration is required if she is at a bar or club with her friends. You need to be aware of social peer pressure. Is she the leader of her group? What emotions would she likely feel just by conversing with you? What will her friends think? Will her self-image increase or decrease by hanging out with you? These are all subconscious things you need to be aware of. Especially in a world that has a big double standard towards sex.

Showing emotional intelligence means you are much more likely to understand why she is behaving a certain way. All people behave differently and you need to calibrate accordingly in order to be relatable. Relatability helps breed comfort and attraction will than stem from this comfort. Even in long term relationships you will likely find your significant other behaving differently due to social pressure. Just by you understanding what the social pressures are will help you to relate to your partner in whatever situations you find yourselves in.

Be Open Minded

Keep an open mind. Being open minded means not shooting down anything without at least contemplating the idea first. When topics come up in your dating lives make sure you don't put down anything you don't have a reason to. Embrace the unknown, don't fear it.

In the dating context, instead of going to a place you have already been to for your second date why not try something spontaneous and out there. Maybe she said she wanted to go to Mongolia so you decide to take her to a random hole in the wall Mongolian restaurant. Do it fearlessly. The more things you try yields more references and stories you have which therein equates to having an easier time conjuring up engaging conversation (S1.4).

People are often too rigid, stuck in their ways and seemingly always want things to go perfectly. It is far better to learn how to act around imperfections. The natural world isn't perfect, everyone has their own motivations and agendas, so don't try to conjure up the perfect date. You should want to be able to see how you, as well as your potential significant other, behave under unusual and conceivably sub-optimal circumstances. Perhaps you go to a Greek restaurant with authentic belly dancers on your second date and she gets mad because you were looking at the belly dancers. Is this the woman you want to spend your life with? She's already speaking to her insecurity of jealousy on a second date and she's already feeling entitled enough to impose that frame on you? She may be the most composed lady but how will she act when you get lost driving on a fun spontaneous road trip? She can blame you, that's fine as you're in the driver seat, but will she help you after the initial blame has been laid? Will she stay positive? Or will her whole day be ruined because you were an hour later than planned? The more open minded you can be earlier on then the further assortment of situations you can throw at each other to see how you both handle certain imperfections.

Reframe anything you haven't done as an opportunity to learn. Way too many guys get stuck and only continue to do what they already know how to do. This comfort is an ego, self-inflicted through the efficiency of specialization. They are afraid to allow themselves to fail. "I never painted, I suck at painting, and so I won't do a paint night date with my girlfriend." You know how many lady's go to paint night with their girlfriends or parents because their boyfriends cant embrace something new? Think of the opportunity for you to look good in front of her friends just by not being insecure about looking bad, going out and trying something new, while building a new reference towards painting.

The opportunities other guy's reactively shoot down without first trying offers a huge area for competitive advantage over them, as well as your previous self. The more open minded you are, the further you branch out into various things to form opinions on. Your identity won't be shut down, stagnant, and afraid to change. Try new things, not because you think they will be good, but purely because you haven't done them before.

Being open minded further allows you to examine situations from multiple viewpoints. This gives you a vantage point many people never have. This open mindedness transcends into being empathetic. Empathy is what makes a good leader a great leader. In the context of dating, it will better allow you to understand your potential significant others viewpoint. This increase in understanding will increase your ability to relate to people, enabling you to create more meaningful relationships with everyone around you.

Furthermore, getting out of your comfort zone by being open minded enables you to be genuinely excited. Use this excited state to make your potential significant other excited too via the

Law of State Transference (S1.5). It is okay to try new things and fail miserably at them. You have to learn to laugh when you fail instead of letting your ego preserve itself through inaction. You don't have to be perfect at everything but you should be perfectly fine with yourself. Ego preservation is a large component of why people fail to keep an open mind. It is actually a function of the ego to try to maintain a sense of being in control so that this level of comfort can be maintained. Your inaction towards something you have never tried should be chalked up to ego preservation. Though if the action itself is life threatening then it could be genuine self-preservation.

The more open minded you are the easier time you will have removing the preservative defense mechanism part of the ego. The longer the ego is in place the harder it will be to move it, especially as you become committed to that identity. In fact, in the worst case scenario, people can build their identity around their ego so much so that if the ego is shattered they also fall apart with it and are no longer able to build themselves back up.

This open mindedness will enable you to be more resourceful for creating conversation, allow you to be fun and exciting and thus allowing for proper use of the Law of State Transference. Holistically, it will also make you a more robust and overall well-rounded individual. The more diversified, seemingly "out there", actions you take, the more resourceful and dependable you will naturally become.

Be Gallant & Chivalrous

Generally, being a gentlemen is always a good idea. The traditional sense of being a gentlemen means giving value but expecting nothing back. It should be demonstrated by offering nice, small gestures that show you care for her. This doesn't mean being misogynistic. Make sure you can easily distinguish the difference. As mentioned in the social macro session there is an increase in assertive feminist mindsets. For example, holding a door for a lady now in 2016 instead of her just saying "thank you" she might say, "I'm strong enough to do it myself, thanks" as she walks right through the door you held open. The act of you holding a door for her implies to that individual that you think it's more likely she's not strong enough than it is likely that you are just being courteous. You can't control what a women thinks of you but you can control what your intention is. So how can you circumvent not being in the way of the rise of assertive feminism but still be a gentlemen?

The best way to meet assertive feminism is to be gallant & chivalrous to both men and women. Take gender out of it. Taking gender out of the equation will make the misogynist frame the female asserted you with in the above example actually cease to exist in your reality. Do you hold the door open to just women or for men as well? Do you hold the door open for her because you think it's just the right thing to do or do you because "her arms are frail and she doesn't have the muscle to open the door herself?"

A misogynist pays for dinner because he expects something in return, likely sex. A gentleman offers to pay for dinner anytime he invites a guest.

A gentleman:

- Opens the car door.

- Offers a jacket when it's cold.

- Offers help with luggage.

- Waits to sit until after everyone else sits.

- Walks closest to the street.

Remember to come from the mind frame that these are just small value giving courtesies. You don't have an agenda or expect anything back for doing them. Individuals of the fairer sex may condemn all of these activities heedlessly and that's just fine. Don't change your behavior because of their potential reaction. Truly believe that none of these courtesies are a slight on feminism. You should agree with equal rights & supporting strong independent women but this doesn't mean forgoing basic gentlemanly offerings.

Don't let assertive feminism kill chivalry.

Respect the "No" Response

Learn from and accept the "No" response. Not taking a rejection personally is easily side-stepped by identifying the ego, coming from a degree of abundance and mastering outcome independence. Simply accepting the "No" and carrying on is the best response. "Failure is an event, not a person." – Zig Ziglar (Renowned Salesmen & Author).

Don't keep pushing a woman that says "No". Out of respect for her, but also out of respect for yourself. Pursuing a woman that says "No", automatically makes you chase, increases her social value and makes it externally look like you need her to say "Yes" for your ego to save face. While those are the dating reasons why you shouldn't, you also shouldn't keep pursuing a woman that says "No" because that's how you end up in a legal mess (stalking, sexual harassment, etc.). DON'T PURSUE A WOMAN THAT SAYS "NO"! Often times just shrugging it off and moving forward, shows you don't care about being rejected which conveys natural ingrained resilience and strength of character. This may in turn incite that lady who just brushed you off to actually do a 180° and approach you later.

This section really should be a no brainer but whenever the ego is involved it needs to be stated. Don't let rejection affect you. You will become naturally indifferent towards it once you have mastered outcome independence.

Giving vs. Taking Mentality

This is really a topic about giving value. Every interaction you have, with anyone really, but with a woman you are interested in especially, is that you should give abundantly but expect nothing in return. Think a bright "hot sun" vs. a "black hole".

The sun is a never ending positive feedback loop that spirals upward. You provide value, making you feel good about yourself, this in turn makes you want to provide more value. What you get back is an individual's smile and appreciation, which you don't even need.

The black hole is a never ending negative feedback loop that spirals downward, taking value from others. The black hole hurts itself by holding in its own energy; in a perverted sense of efficiency and preservation. This efficiency and preservation point of view comes from a deeply ingrained scarcity mentality. Would we need to preserve something if it were abundant? Some black holes are highly educated but take from others due to a logical frame that makes them want to maximize their own efficiency regardless of anyone else. When someone gives value into a black hole the black hole is completely disengaged. What the black hole doesn't understand is that they are not getting one over on another person's generosity. Because, even when they get what they want, they still don't feel better about themselves.

A less extreme black hole believes in a zero sum game, meaning that there can only be one winner and one loser. When you take on this zero sum mentality you can often "win" every battle but still lose the war. This is because you are always creating a loser. If you frame yourself as a manipulator trying to think what you can get out a situation by doing something or giving a gift but expecting something in return, this is a pure example of a zero sum game.

A sun is expansive. A sun would rather give a gift than receive it. As Zig Ziglar wrote in Secrets of Closing the Sale, "You can have everything in life you want, if you will just help other people get what they want." In order to be a sun, the act of giving, in and of itself has to be self-rewarding.

Value doesn't come from material, external things. It doesn't come from the flashiest car, the best job, abs or the biggest paycheck. Value, in the context of attracting a woman, comes from giving away everything you offer with no expectations of reward or recognition. The truth is you already are a high-value man; the trick is just realizing this. Being genuine, unfiltered, able to lead, positive and happy, constantly working on yourself mentally & physically all the while planning for a better future are all ways you provide value. Value is what you bring to the table. Hold nothing back. The sun doesn't.

Women like the sun because it's positive, radiant with energy and pushes no agenda. The sun burns internally and is fueled from within. It does its own thing and brings people along for the ride while firing up and invigorating anyone it comes in contact with. Bring the sun to your relationships. Be the sun.

Like the sun vs. black hole idea, all the Core Social Skills give value. In mastering the Core Social Skills you will already be aligning your behaviour to be more like a sun.

S3 Embrace Technology

Modern dating requires some degree of technological evolvement. The caveat is that technology in and of itself can be a crutch making up for inept social aptitude. Even with various dating platforms and tools I can't name here it is still highly beneficial for you to try cold approaching women. Cold approaching gives you the ability to put yourself out there, express who you are and deal with real, non-preordained social interactions. Cold approach teaches you humility and how to deal with rejection in a public social setting. These social platforms will provide you an alternative means to meet your potential significant other, but will you have obtained the necessary social perception to keep them interested in you in the long run? Will you be able to lead, hold your frame, take no for an answer, identify your ego, remain true to yourself despite your significant others influence and continue to have deep meaningful conversations long after the romantic sunsets? Or will you succumb to the high divorce statistic, being needy, clingy, following her around all the time, compromising your sense of self and purpose, and in the long run making yourself disengaged in order to make her "happy". I cannot underline this point enough. The Core Social Skills at the beginning of this book are critical for the long term success of any relationship. Do not use technology to circumvent the social skills required to build a meaningful relationship. Technology, ironically, while more socially accepted for dating than cold approach is, it is actually more "gamy" in so far that you are both cheating yourself the precious skills required to navigate through life's obstacles. Be it communication, jealousy, neediness, resourcefulness, introspection... all these areas of your relationship would be improved if you work on those Core Social Skills.

That being said, technology does not have to be mutually exclusive to cold approach. You can also use and practice many of those Core Social Skills on these dating platforms (once you meet the individual in person). Dating technology offers many advantages such as the ability to filter through to find people you are attracted to. Technology further provides insight that enables you with the ability to know if that the other person is single and looking for a potential life partner. A double edged sword advantage is that it does help to nullify the social anxiety one would face in a cold approach situation; however, circumventing social anxiety means you may never learn how to deal with it.

These days there are tiers of dating platforms, all with their individual strengths and weaknesses. The first level is your basic dating, mobile, platform. Free, easy to use, very few words and very little investment. The second level is _free_ dating sites that have a real profile page that allow for more content and hobbies and interests. Finally the third level is _paid_ dating sites that have a similar function to the second level but require more initial investment to set up. I have used all these dating sites/platforms so I will go through the pro's and con's of each of them.

S3.1 Basic/Strictly Mobile Dating Platforms

Platforms in this category are typically all pictures with little to no content. I found the primary function of these platforms were more for people that were searching for Mr./Mrs. Right Now as opposed to Mr./Mrs. Right. Not to be pretentious or condescending, I found the quality of people using these platforms to be the lowest and extremely young relative to the other technology tiers. As a 28 year old heavy into self-improvement, school, book writing while working full time I didn't expect to find a life partner on there. That being said using these platforms for a tool for social references was very beneficial which I did use it for. For content for this book, for stories to share with friends and for contrasting what I was looking for with what I wasn't looking for. Now this is debatable and a little harsh, as I actually only went on a few dates from mobile platforms so my sample size is small. With that disclosure in mind I found most "matches" to be very dependent and looking more for a fling than for a relationship. As a word of warning to my younger male readers, building a relationship with a woman that uses mobile platforms to find dates is a little strange. Make no mistake, typically attractive women get approached quite often so the fact they are on free mobile dating application could indicate a constant need for social validation which could correlate into a lower than average self-esteem. Or at least her self-esteem is highly dependent on what other people think. This would hopefully likely change as she gets older but my overall warning here is not to use current mobile dating apps as a resource to build long term relationships.

For success with these platforms make sure to always be yourself. While being genuine is less important on these mobile platforms, given the intention is overall more short term in nature, you can still use them to learn about the different type of women that are out there so that you can make the best decision on who you want to date.

Regarding photos, for all three tiers of technological dating platforms, make sure you are always smiling in your profile photo and try to avoid bathroom selfies. I have been told by countless female sources that a shirtless selfie in the bathroom showing off your abs is repellent. If you do decide on a shirtless picture, know that it conveys cockiness and also know that while it is a good thing you take care of your health, you may be catering to different types of ladies based on your photos. Now this is rare but you may get women that would date you for your body and then when your body changes all of a sudden she won't be around anymore. Make sure any relationship you strive to build is more than skin deep because unfortunately we all age. If you do post a topless picture, make sure the caption is something either funny or something that conveys that you know it is cocky so as not to be seen as socially illiterate. A picture of your full body on a beach during your guy's trip to Cancun is fine. Abs are powerful and do illicit attraction but aren't meant to serve as a reason to date someone, at least on their own. It is better for you to know that she is interested in you before you show her your abs; that way you know she liked you before she knew you had abs so you won't be insecure about losing them. The same thing can be said for money, which ties into the wealth section later. If you do have money, don't flaunt it, make sure she likes you for you before you let on that you have money. That way again, you won't be insecure about it. These facts about yourself should be brought up in a "by the way" blasé manner.

S3.2 Free Dating Sites

Platforms in this category contain additional written content than the strictly mobile tier below it. Like the smaller mobile platforms they are free and you can post photos. However, unlike those smaller strictly mobile platforms you and the lady you are attracted to can list parts of your personality on the page. How filled out the profile is can be a direct indicator of how invested the woman is in finding a partner online. Keep in mind, ideally, the woman probably doesn't want to find someone online. Most ladies would rather meet their partner in a genuine, romantic, spontaneous, "swept off her feet" moment. Online interactions generally removes instantaneous and in the moment emotions which means the bar will be much higher for the type of things you write. Since you have time to write and plan things out, the amount of effort you put in is probably one of the barometers she will use to decide if she wants to meet you.

These free dating sites are a good way to filter down to the women you think you want to get to know based on the personality they put on the page. Make sure you are both physically attracted to the photos as well as to the words she puts on her profile. Keep in mind most women on these sites get multiple messages a day. Mostly just short messages and pick up lines men wouldn't have the gall to use in person. This means you have to stand out... which oddly enough can simply just mean reading her profile and commenting on something you found interesting. Though again, if she receives enough messages, even that effort would be diluted as a number of people would be doing that too. This is one of the biggest pitfalls on free online dating services. A potential way around this con would be to take what she has on her page and reframe it into what it means to you. Due to the sheer volume of messages she receives you need to think creatively and not do what everyone else does.

If you really like the women make sure you don't appear needy online. Constantly messaging her to get back to you is not attractive. A quick way to tell if a woman is just being polite to you is if she is replying with a sentence and you are typing paragraphs.

The leading issues with free dating sites are the fact that some people don't look like their pictures while other's that do aren't actually looking for a relationship; just social validation. Success on free dating sites often mean putting in quite a bit of time just to find someone you genuinely want to meet and then, after that search, putting in the additional effort required to get her comfortable enough to actually meet you.

S3.3 Paid Dating Sites

Paid dating platforms are great sites if you have additional disposable income and not a lot of time to go out and meet people. People on these sites generally don't want to waste time. The fact that everyone pays money to be on the site makes it so that people take finding a potential life partner much more seriously than the alternative non-paid dating sites, which they should, as the decision to find a significant other is one of the biggest decisions in our lives.

These paid sites save time by allowing you to filter using software for "women, who want children, over 5'5, like to keep fit, with a bachelor degree or higher and reside in a specific geographical region." This allows you to target certain people in an extremely efficient matter. Plus the people listed are also mainly looking for a meaningful relationship. I personally used paid dating sites as a tool to find people who also believe in self-improvement and enjoy traveling, being active etc....

The only caveat on these platforms is, like the free sites, that some people may lie about who they are and what they look like. In the long run these individuals fade away as the monetary barrier makes it not really worth their time to be fake in perpetuity. If they are lying on their profile on an online dating website chances are they will have more than their fair share of insecurity so it is best to stay away if you happen to be unfortunate enough to run into those people along the way. I can tell you more than a few funny stories of this happening to me.

For these websites to work effectively you also have to have a high degree of knowledge of what you think you want in a potential life partner. This is why cold approach or even free mobile platforms are beneficial because you can use it as a bench mark for knowing the type of women you want. Additionally, dating a few people at a time online will help you cognitively think about what woman is the right one but most importantly decide what qualities you like/dislike in each of them so that you can keep filtering down further.

Online dating sites have their place in modern dating. If you have additional money and a lack of time I highly suggested the paid websites. Date, shop around, and know for sure what you want by coming from an air of abundance. Don't blind yourself because you haven't been on a date with a cute lady for a while. Pretty women are everywhere. A lovely women who supports you and has all the qualities you want with very little you don't want is rare. Paid dating sites are a quick way to pile on date experience, phone numbers, create references and generate self-confidence that you can leverage off of for your day to day life. All of a sudden because you are more confident in your abilities you won't let that 6'1 blonde model you are extremely attracted to slowly walk out of existence without at least attempting to "man up" and say "hi". Finally, you will also learn a lot about social dynamics. Most importantly you will learn about yourself because you learn the types of things you actually enjoy talking about, as they will have a way of showing up consistently on the various dates you will embark upon. Constant online dates are a way you can easily form a concrete identity or at least become consciously aware of both your personality and your long term goals.

Both free and paid dating sites give you some insight into who you are meeting ahead of time. Make sure you aren't meeting just anyone who replies to you. If you do that it means you believe you deserve whatever lady happens to decide that she is interested in you. Not only does this associate with low self-esteem but it also makes you reactionary and desperate. This desperation will bring up red flags for her like why other women don't seem to be that into you.

When you start online dialogue make sure you have read her profile a few times and build up your comfort before giving your number online or taking the interaction forward "offline". Use basic common sense when meeting strangers on the internet. Now when I say read her page I mean not just the words on her profile but also how she structured her page. What does she want you to see? How does she come across? Before you meet her you should have an awareness that you truly believe she could have the potential be a good long term partner for you or not. If not you are really just wasting her time and yours.

After making your mind up on meeting the woman you are interested in use her profile to your advantage. Remember, unlike cold approach, she agreed to meet you so you don't have the burden that exists (for whatever reason) that shames a guy for approaching a woman and telling her he is attracted to her. That being said, because you are not on the spot you have time to plan out the things you want to say so the benchmark from her point of view will be higher. Many guys simply don't put in the extra effort when meeting a woman for the first time. This extra effort is talking in terms of the other person's interest. Now this is a bit backwards from the "talk about what you find interesting" mantra mentioned in the engaging conversation, S1.4 Core Social Skill topic. This swap occurs because the situation is now structured as a date and you already have an idea of who she is so you can instead talk about things that interest her. Obviously be genuine about this. If you don't care about the things she finds interesting, don't fake it for your own social validation. Talking about the things she finds interesting on the first date is an easy way to understand what you are getting into and ensure you make the best decision for yourself if you do decide to pursue a relationship with her.

But how do you make sure not to run out of things to talk about on the first date if you are not interested in the things she likes?

1.) Leverage off the profile page. Do a small amount of research on the types of things she likes and interests she has, as she has a profile page full of them. Why is it that anyone whom was ever a guest of former US President Theodore Roosevelt amazed at the sheer range of his knowledge? The answer is whenever Roosevelt expected a visitor he stayed up late reading up on the subject in which he saw his guest was particularly interested. Why not take a page out of a man much smarter than I and do your due diligence before you meet someone. This small effort shows you care about what you're getting into even before you really meet them. This early investment in them will make them want to invest back in you, especially after they are already invested enough to be sitting across from you. Obviously don't go overboard in your research as that would appear crazy, creepy or try hard. Hopefully, her page had a few hooks that you are at least semi-interested in or else why would you ask her to meet you? Make sure you don't frame this research as "gamy". This is not manipulation unless you are falsely aligning your interests with her. You should frame this extra research as just wanting to see if you can be interested in the things she is.

2.) If all else fails and conversation wanes, well past the point of planned pauses, the next best thing is to resort to talking about your interests instead. In cold approach this should be your go-to anyway. If you decided to circumvent approaching strangers & conveying interest then talking about yourself might be hard for you. Not being able to talk about what interests you reveals a lack of cognitive identity. If someone asked "who are you?" You might not know or you might just associate with your job. Your job isn't who you are. Your identity is not your job. It is not what you do, it is who you are. However, the emotions behind how you do your job could be part of your identity. Repeated exposure in talking about your interests with strangers will actually strengthen your self-image which will therein make your confidence increase. Dating is like a muscle and will actually get easier the more you go on dates and introduce yourself to strangers.

One of the questions you should ask her at the start of a date is if she has gone on many online dates before. Chances are she probably will have. If she "pleads guilty" to more than a few, try to talk less about the same things other people would have. That is, it is generally advisable to talk about yourself in this scenario instead of her, as she might be tired of telling the same basic stories every time she meets an online date in person. I always found it interesting to ask what she thought about me going into the date based on my profile. Typically I always asked questions I genuinely wanted to know answers to. If I didn't care about her pet lizard I didn't ask what it ate, how long she had it for or where she got it from. Remember the first few dates aren't interviews. Keep the conversation light and fun and don't ring out question after question. Women can be just as bad as guys at this and I always found it fun to call them out on it. Just telling a lady, "when will the interview process be over so I can see if I got the job?" is the best way to make her stop barraging you with questions or at least hopefully save the next guy from an onslaught of inquisition. Though, in hindsight, I think I liked saying that line more just to see how she would handle that assertion. Remember don't use canned material, review Core Social Skill S1.4, let her talk about herself, and never be afraid to state what you really think. Being genuine is the key to building comfort and attraction.

To set up your first date always lead. Be open to "rejection." Pick an exact time and venue with bonus points if you can link it to a venue she implied she might like to try during the initial online conversation. Usually your only pre-screen question would be what side of the city she resides on so you get an idea what is logistically easy for her. If she wants to meet you but is busy she will work with you. If she doesn't want to meet you then chances are the reply will be short and unhelpful. Don't take it personally, some women simply don't like to flat out say "No" online. Perhaps they just don't want to meet you but are too "polite" to turn you down. Perhaps it's because they already found someone. Perhaps they just don't want to terminate any further potential external validation i.e. chasing. Whatever the case, which you will never truly know, don't get hung up pondering over it. Move on and keep being yourself.

Some tips for setting up a profile:

Try to be memorable but still yourself. You do this by being polarizing. Instead of my self-summary reading:

"I am an introverted accountant."

It could read "I am just extroverted enough to do karaoke after a beer or two which speaks volumes as a stereotypical introverted accountant."

Make sure your profile reads more like a kid's picture book than a novel. Think of what you are trying to get across and what a random stranger who reads it quickly is likely to picture in their head. In my profiles I tried to combat the "introverted accountant" stereotype with as much random things I could think of that I had fun doing. This made an easy polarity paradigm which you just integrate and weave in and out of consistently in your profile. "Doing spreadsheets by day, shooting gun's at the shooting range via online dates by night... being an accountant is hella tight." Now instead of just a typical accountant we have a not so typical account that shoots guns and isn't "too" afraid of karaoke. Basically they shouldn't know exactly what they are getting into, leave some mystery to make them want to meet you and at the same time not compromise yourself in the process. In your profile go over what each sentence is saying about yourself from a stranger's point of view and second what the overall message of your profile is. Remove or alter anything that isn't clear or isn't congruent with who you are. More information generally isn't better but you do need enough content to illustrate some degree of effort.

It is highly advisable to supplement your online dating with cold approaching people you are interested in pursuing romantically. This mitigates the greatest con that utilizing technology brings forth: situational confidence. You need internal confidence in your relationships and the only way to have internal confidence in dating and asserting genuine interest is by approaching strangers. Doing so ensures you are not circumventing the Core Social Skills advocated at the beginning of this book. Remember these Core Social Skills exist to ensure longevity of relationships. Technology is a situational crutch and should be viewed as a tool utilized on the side, while still developing your ongoing social capacity. Paid dating sites are a great way to assist you in overcoming scarcity, helping to verify that you come from a place of abundance when selecting a partner for life. Just don't make the mistake of relying on it.

S4 - Common Mistakes in Dating

I am not a big fan of "what not to do" lists, but I did make one due to the fact that some people learn from what to do and some people learn better from what not to do. If you learn better from what not to do lists you should reflect on why that is as it may be you have a slightly biased negative tendency. Regardless, below are some common mistakes I ran into and took note of during my dating life. I say common, not because I think you may have them, but because I still struggle with these mistakes even today. Constant self-improvement means having to accept constant drawbacks. The development of an ego is a large component of these mistakes. The value of this list is that you can identify with these mistakes and then you can begin to climb out of these pitfalls quicker because you are more aware of them.

1.) <u>Playing not to lose</u>. This ties into division of intent and is a direct violation of a Core Social Skill. This occurs mainly due to ego preservation. Not everyone has to like you and they don't know you enough anyway to really reject you. Playing not to lose converts into meaning you don't want to win. It means holding back and not giving it your all. The sun doesn't hold back.

2.) <u>Impulsive Ejection</u>. This ties into the first mistake with ego preservation. When you get a good reaction don't just randomly leave. If you suffer from leaving a positive interaction early it means you are after people validating you. Unless you really are after a gold star on your fridge, instead of a potential life partner, don't bail out of a conversation early.

3.) <u>Not going out</u>. This is probably my worst mistake. Convincing myself I'll go out next weekend or tomorrow instead of tonight. At one time I thought I needed a house or abs in order to feel worthy of going up to a stranger and saying "hi". Even with a house I found I still felt "unworthy" of going up to anyone much less a lady I was attracted to. This sense of self-worth cannot be attained through any material or alternative means and it shouldn't. It shouldn't because a relationship can't be built on "if you have a house or not". Any external good will not make you more valuable in the context of building a meaningful relationship. If the only reason you're comfortable approaching a woman is because you have material things it means you rely on something that doesn't come from within. In the long run it is much better to go out, be a little unsure, take action and learn by doing whilst being yourself. That is the only way you will truly know how you come across, get confidence from the social references and improve your ability to naturally calibrate. Then, when you see that one woman you are head over heels for you have the audacity to get up, approach her and let her know exactly how you are feeling. Taking action is the only way to improve.

4.) <u>Not leading</u>. Leading should feel natural. It means you know where you are going and you want (not need) people to come with you. It also means never saying, "I don't know, what do you want to do?" This kills attraction and makes both people have to think logically about planning, taking away from being in the moment. Recall you don't need to be correct when you lead but you do need to lead. Sometimes the best answer for leading is just taking a direction and walking, especially in any non-serious social setting. Not leading can also be an indicator that you aren't interested in what's around you or aren't cognitive enough to take any affirmative action.

5.) Trying to <u>impress other people</u>. Instead just try to talk about what you find interesting and amusing so that the woman gets to see you and your reality. She is interested in what you find interesting, not what <u>you think she wants</u> you to be interested in.

6.) Erroneously trying to <u>take something</u> away from an interaction instead of adding value. You read all these self-help books, got a good job, are financial stable and now you think the world owes you something. This is the epitome of ego but it can also come across as a leeching mentality, which is just as bad. In every relationship you have you should give. Give positive emotions to everyone, even if they just take and never give back. You don't need them to give you positive emotions back. If you come across someone who only takes value, you will know by coming in with a positive mindset. It is likely you will feel exhausted after just hanging out with them for a few hours. Make sure you are not a taker. The simplest and most effective way to never be a taker is never needing anything from anyone. Self-reliant, self-supportive, self-enriched. It's good to have friends or a partner that you can rely on in times of need but don't expect to rely on their support and don't make a habit of using their support.

Concentrate your cognitive ability on the ten Core Social Skills. Utilize the training wheels and tips in the non-core social skills if you need some more self-assurance. The tips enclosed in this section serve to promote awareness and improve overall understanding of what you are likely to run into during your pursuit for a meaningful long term relationship. Additionally, most of the tips do align with one or two of the Core Social Skills, meaning that if you are struggling you may find steps to improve on them in the above non-essential section. For example if you constantly find yourself in a "friend zone" then a pick up line from the outset would be a sure way to convey intention.

Utilize technology at your own judgement based on your circumstance. As long as you continue to take action and throw yourself physically at social situations you will continue to improve socially.

No one said finding a partner for life would be easy, but it's sure as hell one of the most important endeavours you can pursue. It warrants your cognitive decision. Relationships form the intricate underlying foundation in all the significant choices in our lives. Take action. Don't leave it to chance.

PILLAR #2: HEALTH

To segue from the Social Pillar into the Health Pillar, I'll start off with the controversial question of seemingly utmost importance:

Do looks matter?

This question could be in the Social core section, it's even an opener you could use on a group of women if you are feeling too nervous to be direct.

The short answer is yes, looks matter, but only to an extent. Obviously a woman has attraction and standard thresholds, just like a guy. It's just that a guy has more weighting on the looks component of attraction. There are countless sample tests showing more guys agreeing on which woman is hotter when you show them an array of pictures of women. In contrast, a random sample of women voting on the hottest guy's results in a wider degree of distribution.

While this has yet to be scientifically proven with any degree of certainty women's votes are more evenly distributed while guys apparently suffer from group think (similar decision on who the hottest woman was). Why is that? Is there no personality on a picture? Maybe Women are looking at his composure and body position? His smile? How he holds himself?

So while looks do matter should you stress out over them? No.

What should you do to master your health and increase your overall attractiveness?

The above is a loaded question. This book is about you and in the process of bettering yourself, attracting a potential life partner. Understanding that is pivotal in making sure you work out and live a healthy lifestyle <u>for yourself</u> and not for attracting a woman. Work out for the right reasons and not for external validation that can be taken away as quickly as it is given. Come from the mindset that you are working out for yourself, instead of working out for others. This shift is fundamental in your efforts to stick with your commitment to living a healthy lifestyle in the long run.

The first step in bettering yourself is to write a list separating the things you can control about your body from the things you can't. Focus on the health goals you can influence. You can't change how your facial features look... well, I guess you can these days but let's not get into plastic surgery. You can however change your body fat composition, your muscle definition, and even your body posture.

The second step is identifying the things about your body you are insecure about. Then combine the results of steps 1 and 2 to detect which insecurities you can control and those you cannot. How can you create a plan of action to overcome those insecurities? For example, if you are insecure about the fat on your body and face how will you plan to fix that?

Certain insecurities can't be actively rectified. It is far superior to accept and master them. An example of this would be balding. Often times it's better to accept that you are losing your hair and shave your head instead of trying a comb over, wearing a hat and constantly being afraid a woman is going to say something mean when she notices. You're balding, deal with it, don't hide it and above all don't be ashamed of it. Eventually the woman you like will find out your "secret" so don't lie to yourself, take action, and control your insecurities before they control you.

Embracing an insecurity you can't readily fix means being okay with who you are. Accept what you can't change and don't fight it. By showing acceptance you automatically reframe that insecurity as being a part of you, instead of a part of you that you are rejecting. This act will remove that internal turmoil leading to an overall sense of relief and even freedom. This is not an easy thing to do. Accepting an insecurity means accepting that you are not perfect. If you have a strong ego you will not be able to do this.

But what about for an insecurity you can change?

Like the insecurities you can't change you could attempt to accept those insecurities; however, a part of you will always know you could fix those insecurities. This awareness that you could be better but are not taking action to do so will "gnaw" at you. You will likely become defensive and even more insecure about the insecurities you can directly influence. This means they will start eating at you more because you know you could be doing something about them but are "actively" not taking action.

In today's society, the staggering influence of cheap junk food and the general push that "consumerism will make you happy" has led to an obesity epidemic. That is the main insecurity most people deal with today are body weight and image issues. Ultimately, if you take anything away from the Social core section it is that your emotions should come from within; not from any external source. If happiness does come from a cheeseburger, which many modern commercials claim, this means that a simple cheeseburger has direct control over your emotions. It also means that you can "buy happiness" for $3 at your local fast food provider and as we know, you can't buy happiness, so don't lie to yourself. Synthetic happiness due to consumerism is not true happiness if you can't self-generate the emotion. It goes to follow, if you can't self-generate an emotion how can you hope to bring these emotions out of you when you are meeting a women you are interested in pursuing?

The two main avenues to build a better body and overcome most body-related insecurities are nutrition and exercise.

So do you want to lose weight or build muscle?

These avenues are not entirely mutually exclusive until you get to a lower body fat percentage. If you have a high body fat percentage you can actually achieve both simultaneously, at least initially. If you are already fairly healthy this section will still be useful due to the various links proper health maintenance has to social interactions.

For example, in regards to the social implications; two years ago I was 210 pounds and now weigh 150 pounds. I have more confidence, better posture, more stamina and have an overall higher sense of self-worth simply due to losing all that extra fat. Additionally, your body can be seen as a visual indicator of just how much you are improving. Changes that you can physically see are understandably more encouraging in nature. You can constantly see in this book that I attack many social narratives, like consumerism, but the health industry stance is actually correct. A healthier version of you will lead to a better lifestyle. So use this mainstream stance on an active lifestyle as an umbrella for your personal self-improvement goals.

This Health section does assume a degree of equipment which can be found at most gyms. This means you will likely have to overcome gym intimidation to get there. The gym is a great place to get social momentum, get you active and get you taking affirmative action for both short and long term betterment. So why is it so intimidating? No one is judging you half as much as you are judging yourself. The gym is a venue for social improvement, which means you should feel right at home there. No one is going to walk up and call you names. The act of working out is an admittance that you are not perfect. By extension anyone else who is working out for the long run is also likely not to have an ego, you may even find other gym goers supportive. Unlike social anxiety that occurs from going up to a woman you are attracted to for the first time, gym intimidation does wane off once you go to the gym a few times. This is mainly because the gym is constant. You go there and you know what is going to happen. When you walk up to a woman and convey your interest you never know what will happen. Therefore, going to the gym during non-peak hours will help make you comfortable there thus alleviating most of your anxiety overtime. Additionally this anxiety, unlike social anxiety, is likely never to come back to the same degree, even when switching gyms.

Besides going to the gym during non-busy hours having a general "game plan" of what you are going to do when you get there is another may to provide yourself some self-assurance. Enclosed in this Health section is a generic "plan of action" you could follow that will provide confidence in knowing what part of your body you want to attack when you get to the gym. Gym intimidation will be greatly reduced just by doing the above seemingly small things.

A third option to reduce gym intimidation is enlisting in a gym partner. Deciding to enlist a gym partner to go with is up to you. Unlike the two other options it is surprisingly not suggested, at least not entirely. A part time, situational gym partner once a week for some parts of your workout is preferred over having a constant gym companion. Remember the wingman section in the social portion of this book. Don't rely on your wingman in a gym setting, just like you wouldn't rely on your wingman in a social setting. Motivation should come first from within. You need to be self-reliant. What would happen if your wingman suddenly decides to bail on you? Does this mean you can't go to the gym by yourself? If so then your wingman is a crutch. The primary goal at the gym is to work out, not to be social. Therefore don't waste your scarce time allocated to the Health Pillar talking to your gym partner. A gym partner is generally only a good idea when you need a spotter for safety. It is better to reframe everyone in the gym as your potential gym partner.

Ideally, if you have mastered the Core Social Section, you should have no problem asking a guy who is currently not busy for a hand because you, "Never bench pressed 180 lbs before but you've been stuck on 4 sets of 8 reps at 170 lbs for a while and want to give it a try ". If you feel like the potential spotter would judge you for asking for help then you still have a ways to go to be the best version of you. No one cares what you lift, only your ego. You do you, unashamed, with a smile, and they would be more than happy to help you out; especially if you asked politely. Again don't go to the gym with a gym partner. Rather, reframe all people there as a potential gym partner.

Society is behind you when you decide to exercise; unlike society's view on some of the controversial comments in the social section. Utilize society's approval in this case. In my experience when meeting new people, mentioning that you work out is always welcomed with open arms. This allows one to naturally start on the topic of self-improvement, which many of you will be passionate about. This will bring the woman into your point of view and lifestyle under the protection of a mainstream social narrative. Moreover, this translates into a much easier time getting a woman to see you are constantly working on yourself as the changes you are undertaking are visual in nature. Ultimately, the string of events listed above are contingent on that fact that you actually do put the time in and work out. Don't lie to yourself or to the woman in order to manipulate a positive reaction. Finally, don't brag about working out. You don't need external social validation. Work out for yourself.

As mentioned in the Social section, all women are uniquely different. Everyone's body is different as well. Just like when you calibrate to make the woman you are seeing comfortable, make sure you dial in and listen to your own body too. This serves as a disclaimer that what worked for me may not work for you. Don't lie to yourself. Hold yourself accountable to your own personal health goals. "Life ain't a track meet, it's a marathon" – Ice Cube (Well-known Rapper and Actor); Lyrics from "You Can Do It". The only person who can tell if you put in 100% as opposed to 80% is you.

H1 Diet

As a further disclaimer I am by no means a nutrition expert but I can share with you the actions I took in order to drop 60 pounds.

The materials you will need to track and quantify your fitness progress are a scale, a pen and a journal. These materials are important as they serve to take the emotion out of your fitness goals. The scale won't lie in the long term but your brain can. I generally don't like to talk in absolutes when it comes to the human body, since everyone is different, but I guarantee that on a diet your brain will attempt to trick you into rationalizing eating more. And you can't blame it. Eating less than what you burn off will overtime lead to starvation and the human body is amazing in its hardwired ability for self-preservation. To overcome this hardwired disposition you need discipline and a pen and journal in order to track your progress and prove to yourself that you actually are consistently improving.

After reading this section, go out and buy a basic tape measure that you can wrap around your waist. Each day I challenge you to measure your waist and weigh yourself on a scale. When weighing yourself, do it every morning right after you wake up. This will give a more reliable reading with less day to day volatility due to eating & water consumption.

Below is an excerpt from my own "weight loss journal" to give you an example of how to fill in your journal:

May 23, 2016 – Wt: 153.6; waist navel: 31 1/8 Inch

May 24, 2016 – Wt: 153.3; waist navel: 31 1/8 Inch

May 25, 2016 – Wt: 153.5; waist navel: 31 1/8 Inch

....

June 25, 2016 - Wt: 151.2; waist navel 30 7/8 Inch

Moreover, each Friday you should measure your Chest, Hips, Bicep/Tricep, Quads and Calves. This allows you to tell if you are losing weight in the right place (the waist) by contrasting your waist measurements with these measurements.

An example of your Friday entry would be:

June 24, 2016 Wt: 150.8; Waist Navel 30 Inch ±

Chest: 39 ¼ inch; Waist Hips: 34 ¼ Inch; Bicep Right: 13 7/8 Inch; Bicep Left: 14 Inc; Left Thigh: 19 Inch; Calves 13 5/8 Inch.

....

This supplementary weekly measurement of your muscles helps to confirm where you are likely losing the weight, which can became quite critical once you start getting lean. The tape measure helps to serve as a safeguard, giving you the peace of mind that you are maintaining your muscle mass while dieting since your body has overall less fat stores to draw from. This peace of mind is important. As mentioned the brain will try to play tricks on you and it will attempt to rationalize that you are losing too much muscle. If your muscle measurements ever decrease more than your waist you should attempt to figure out why.

Finally, each week you should calculate what percentage of your weight you lost. First, average your weekly weight measurement. Once you have this number, subtract the previous week's average from it. Then divide that total by the prior week weight measurement.

For example:

Week prior average weight = 190.8

Current Week average weight = 189.9

Body weight lost as a percentage = (189.9-190.8)/190.8 = 0.47%

This 0.47% of body weight lost is a metric useless by itself. Therefore, it's suggested you enlist personal targets of body weight to lose each week. In my specific case my personal target was to lose between 0.5% to 1% of my weight per week. I found anything less than that discouraging and anything more than that risked losing my muscle mass (especially when I weighed under 165 pounds).

So now that a system of tracking your progress is in place, it is time for me to answer what you really want to know...

How did I start actually losing weight from a dieting perspective?

As much as the health industry might hate me... losing fat (for me) wasn't from any special diet or meal plan. And it wasn't from any cardiovascular exercises either.

Instead, all I did was count calories. Now this is probably easier for me to do as an accountant but you definitely don't need an accounting designation to count calories. The first step was to remove all non-diet pop and juice; switching to water, coffee and tea for almost all of my fluid intake. Back when I was 210 pounds this switch alone helped reduce my weight. If I had to pick a diet strategy that is out there today mine would be most in line with the intermittent fasting diet; although I did not know this at the time. I found this counting calorie diet the easiest to understand. The logic was solely structured around the idea that what I put into my body had to be less than what my body burned throughout the day. It is now common knowledge that a pound of body fat is composed of approximately 3,500 calories. If I wanted to lose a pound of fat a week I should aim for 3,500 caloric deficit in a week which is 500 calories short a day. I did this. And I stayed with it for 78 weeks.

H1.1 How to Count Calories & Maintain a Caloric Deficit

The act of counting calories is actually fairly straightforward. To be clear I am a big supporter of healthier foods but when I started dieting I lived alone and quite frankly, could not easily afford it. Healthier foods, additionally, are usually much harder to accurately account for caloric intake. For example, not all apples are created equal but "Google" tends to come to the conclusion that an apple is only 52 calories. Given my living situation, lack of time to cut and measure food items, and overall bachelor lifestyle I used TV dinners and whey protein as my main fuel sources. These sources of fuel had the approximate calories labeled on the container which made it very easy to add up. My brain could not find a way to convince me to eat more because I knew almost exactly how many calories I was eating each and every day. That's how I really lost 60 pounds. That being said, I took an array of supplements, which I will get into later, as many of those TV dinners are processed and consequently lack essential nutrients.

Here is the tricky part. How much does your body burn off each day? Everyone's body is different. That's what makes all three Pillars of this book amazing. You never know what the outcome will be but you have a general idea of how things should turn out. Even investments, which are discussed later are really an interaction of people in a marketplace and can be subject to behavioural anomalies just like individual people. So while there are exceptions, the following chart is a general guideline for most people. Please note, this doesn't take into account your physical frame (narrow frame, etc.) but is really based on averages. As a side note, I found that any time physical frames were included, people often lied to themselves to better serve their ego. Consequently, it follow that this schedule just takes into account sex, height, weight and age. A.K.A. things you can't lie to yourself about. This schedule is what I used to determine a baseline caloric intake level (I am 5'10). Instead of using maintenance as a generic baseline, I took out the effect of exercise and attempted to calculate the basic metabolic rate. This basic metabolic rate is what I would burn assuming no extra movement which I found most accurate with a desk job and gave me a margin of safety when losing weight to account for physical activity volatility. This denied my brain the opportunity to manipulate my eating habits. I knew with certainty that eating this amount each day would lower my weight as the amounts listed on the next page assume zero physical activity.

Each day target of calories (Eat less than # on table):

WEIGHT/ HEIGHT*	5'8	5'10	5'11	6
210	1,904	1,936	1,952	1,968
205	1,881	1,913	1,929	1,945
200	1,859	1,890	1,906	1,922
195	1,836	1,868	1,883	1,900
190	1,813	1,845	1,861	1,877
185	1,790	1,822	1,838	1,854
180	1,768	1,799	1,815	1,831
175	1,745	1,778	1,794	1,808
170	1,721	1,754	1,770	1,788
165	1,700	1,730	1,747	1,763
160	1,677	1,709	1,724	1,740
155	1,654	1,686	1,702	1,716
150	1,630	1,663	1,679	1,695
145	1,609	1,640	1,656	1,672
140	1,586	1,618	1,632	1,650

*This schedule is based on a male, age 28, with little to no physical activity. Additionally the above assumes an average Joe bodyweight composition. Muscle does burn more calories to maintain than fat does. This information comes from Freedieting.com and serves as a rough estimate. You can insert some of your personal metrics on this free calculator: http://www.freedieting.com/tools/calorie_calculator.htm to assist you in targeting a caloric intake goal that's right for you.

You can see just by the sheer list of variables and assumptions for said variables the degree of difference between each person. That being said the 5'10 column illustrated is what I used to drop 60 pounds within approximately 78 weeks. Using this chart as a guideline or base framework can help ensure your weight loss goal never stagnates. For example, when I was 5'10 at 185 pounds, eating less than 1822 calories daily would ensure I would start losing weight overtime. Then when I hit 180 lbs I would drop to eating less than 1799 calories a day. The only time I struggled to lose weight was mentally. Especially when people started commenting that I was "losing weight too quickly" and that I was becoming too light for my height, both of which were "unhealthy". Everyone is entitled to their opinions when it comes to a healthy body. Maybe they had my best interest at heart or maybe they were projecting their own self-image on me. In life you will find that many friends don't actually want you to change. They like who you are now, that is why they are your friend, and any change might alter things with them. It doesn't mean they are a bad friend but it can get in the way of self-improvement. That being said I decided to ask my doctor what weight for my body specifically would be considered unhealthy and he said approximately 128 pounds... which is much lower than I would ever want to achieve anyway. This gaping disparity between the doctor and common feedback I was receiving from peers could indicate a potential disconnect between what society vs. the doctor view as unhealthy. Reframe anyone who says you should stop losing weight into that they are just trying to look out for you. Do not get defensive; frame it as appreciation of your results. You know what your targets are and if you are unsure if you are targeting a healthy weight, ask a doctor. Not knowing will leave you in limbo as it provides a way for your brain to tell you to eat more. Speaking of doctors, remember, I am by no means a doctor and most importantly I am not you. If you have any health complications you should always consult your doctor before you decide to take any drastic lifestyle changes. Dieting and exercise is a lifestyle change; especially when your body is used to excess.

It is suggested for weight loss to have a dual mandate of waist size coupled with your overall weight target goal. Hitting the weight target will likely be easier than hitting a waist target. You would likely have to drop to a lower weight than you think to achieve that "30 inch waist" for that 6 pack. A dual mandate helps measure that you are indeed losing more fat than muscle and also aligns with the motivational ab target. How to set a target waist size is contingent on your frame (hips), how developed your core is and what your body fat percentage target is. A strong measure of overall fitness, athleticism and aesthetics is derived from a lower body fat percentage.

H1.2 Determining Body Fat Percentage

There are a variety of tools out there like Calipers, Bioelectric Impedance, Hydrostatic weighting and the DEXA scan that work to measure your body fat percentage. That being said, most of these take money, technology, time and usually someone else to help take more accurate readings. I found this below chart to be a fairly good indicator of your overall body fat percentage. Abs will generally not show above 14% body fat and for most people the percent that is likely to reveal abdominals is around 10-12% body fat.

Body Fat %	General Waist Measurement*
5-6% bf	Waist is 41.8% of height. If 5'10 = 170Cm * 41.8% = 71.06 cm =28.0 Inch Waist
6-7% bf	Waist is 42.1% of height. If 5'10 = 170Cm * 42.1% = 71.57 cm =28.2 Inch Waist
7-8% bf	Waist is 42.5% of height. If 5'10 = 170Cm * 42.5% = 72.25 cm =28.5 Inch Waist
8-9% bf	Waist is 43.0% of height. If 5'10 = 170Cm * 43.0% = 73.10 cm =28.9 Inch Waist
9-10% bf	Waist is 43.6% of height. If 5'10 = 170Cm * 43.6% = 74.12 cm =29.2 Inch Waist
10-12% bf	Waist is 44.7% of height. If 5'10 = 170Cm * 44.7% = 75.99 cm =29.9 Inch Waist
12-14% bf	Waist is 45.7% of height. If 5'10 = 170Cm * 45.7% = 77.69 cm =30.6 Inch Waist

*These measurements would be skewed if one has a highly developed core. Again this is a rough approximation. This table is slightly tweaked but originates from Radu Antoniu's observation of targeting a specific waist size and estimating body fat percentage by using waist as a percent of height. Radu Antoniu is another recommended YouTube persona and author at Think Eat Lift (Fitness Blog).

For the average reader, using waist as a percentage of your height is a good way to estimate your body fat percentage without investing in tools. This chart assumes a male gender and uses a height of 5'10 to supply a base example. If your goal was to get abs you would aim for 10-12% body fat.

Using myself as an example, in order to determine my target waist size to achieve my personal abs goal you would follow these steps:

Step 1: Convert height to centimeters: 5'10" = 170cm.

Step 2: Multiply centimeters by 44.7% (this is the number in the table for a target of 10-12% body fat) =75.99cm

Step 3: Convert the result into inches: 75.99cm = 29.92". This is your target waist measurement around the navel.

The above is a lose indicator of body fat percentage. Tools are more accurate but they cost resources. The ab target in and of itself can be used as a finite visual indicator for determining when to stop focusing on dieting and when to start focusing on gaining muscle. It follows that when your abs are revealed you have a lower body fat percentage. Therefore you can utilize abs themselves as a barometer to determine when you are beginning to eat too much. If you are eating too much then your abs will stop showing. This visual indicator can't lie, unlike your brain during an overly generous lean bulk phase which will attempt to justify eating more and more "to gain muscle"... potentially undoing the hard weeks of dieting you just put yourself through.

H1.3 Supplements

Below is a list of supplements recommended to ensure your body gets the essential nutrients you are unable to get when dieting. It follows that on a diet you are less likely to get the optimal amount of nutrients so therefore supplements are suggested.

- Vitamin D – The body naturally produces Vitamin D provided there is an adequate amount of UV light from sun exposure. That being said, anyone with a desk job could have a very hard time ensuring an optimal level of Vitamin D is attained. Optimal Vitamin D levels lend to a normal functioning immune system and are essential for the development of healthy bones and teeth. If you are Vitamin D deficient, which is quite different than just not being at an optimal level, than natural testosterone levels will suffer.

- Fish Oil – Both kinds of Omega 3 acids – Eicosapentaenoic acid (EPA) & Docosahexaenoic acid (DHA). Fish oil is highly recommended if you eat lots of red meat and eggs which is common in the current pro-protein era of body building. Having Omega 3 acids helps counteract the side effects of eating too much Omega 6 acids (red meat & eggs) and therefore the fish oil supplement works to help stabilize this imbalance.

- Vitamin C – Given during a diet one is consuming less, this means your body is likely utilizing fewer resources as its metabolic rate slows. This could compromise your immune system. Vitamin C has been shown to help boost the immune system and promote the healing of wounds. This vitamin serves as a safe way to help make yourself less susceptible to sickness at a time where your body has less resources to work with.

- Creatine Monohydrate- This is more for weight lifting than dieting but it is a supplement highly useful in increasing lean body mass. When muscles start contracting, Adenosine Triphosphate (ATP) utilizes a phosphate to power the contraction. The ATP then becomes Adenosine Diphosphate (ADP) which is "useless" as far as we are concerned until creatine replaces the phosphate so that ADP becomes ATP again. The more creatine readily available, the more times your muscles can contract, given a fixed period of time. Reframe the function of creatine as a bunch of mechanics waiting for the race car to pull in for a pit stop. The more creatine in your body, the more mechanics you have available which, in theory, should get the car (your muscle) back on the race track quicker. This supplement then enables someone to pump out more sets/reps and lends itself to high volume endurance training. Creatine Monohydrate has also shown to increase water muscle retention which may assist you in lifting heavier weights as your body itself will be heavier.

- Whey Protein Isolate – It is suggested to take approximately 0.8 grams of whey protein per pound of body weight when dieting and up that to 1 gram to 1.2 grams per pound of body weight when starting to shift focus from weight loss to muscle building. That is, if you weigh 180 pounds and are dieting you should be taking roughly 144 grams of protein per day. Protein is essential in order to repair the muscle after you tear it during your work out. Please note that protein only needs to be supplemented if you are working out, but any good diet should have a component of weight lifting to ensure your body is optimally targeted to remove fat as opposed to muscle for its energy source. If the body thinks it needs to keep its muscle it is more likely to cannibalize fat as an energy source rather than muscle.

In general, any traditional multivitamin is also recommended. A multivitamin is a good way to ensure that your body isn't deficient in any of the 24 essential nutrients while following a diet. Everyone's diet will be different so you will likely need to supplement your diet differently. For example, I personally also used calcium supplements. This is mainly because I found the foods I cut the most, especially when trying to lose those final few pounds, happened to be high in calcium. The world supplement means to <u>add to</u> something. This means supplements are not meant to be standalone sources of any nutrient in the long run. Tailor the supplements you need to your own diet.

H1.4 Intermittent Fasting

As mentioned briefly within the Health Pillar introduction, the diet structure I used, besides counting calories, was what people call "Intermittent Fasting". You will likely find that counting calories naturally lends itself to an intermittent fasting strategy. The underlying content in this small section originates from author and YouTube persona Greg O-Gallagher.

So what exactly is intermittent fasting and why might it be beneficial?

First, you have to understand the difference between two states: the fed state and the fasted state.

Your body is typically in the fed state when it's processing and absorbing food. The fed state starts when you begin eating and lasts for approximately three to six hours as your body digests the food you just ate. During this fed state it is difficult for your body to burn fat because your insulin levels are high.

In between approximately 6 to 12 hours after eating your body still has elevated levels of insulin but the levels begin decreasing as your body is no longer processing a meal.

Because the human body does not generally enter the fasted state until approximately 12 hours after our last meal that is approximately the time when our insulin levels are low enough that the body starts tapping into its fat storage to generate the energy required to carry out basic metabolic functions.

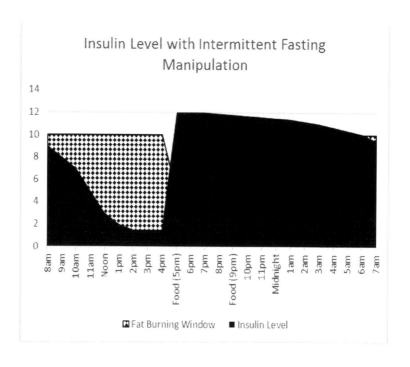

Insulin Level with Intermittent Fasting Manipulation

Fat Burning Window   ■ Insulin Level

In the above example there is a window from 9pm until 5pm (20 hours) where there is no eating. This is my own personal example. Most intermittent fasting windows are typically 12-16 hours in length, but I find the above works best for my current lifestyle. Come from the frame that high insulin levels resemble a physical wall preventing your body from tapping into its fat reserves for energy. The more time your body has to tap into its fat reserves the more it is likely to do so.

Remember I am not your dietitian, your nutrient expert, or your doctor. The following is the schedule I used in order to be successful with my own weight loss goals as a 28 year old healthy male:

Schedule:

6:30 - 10 AM: Drink nothing but water, take vitamins. I found sparkling water to be more filling.

10 AM – Noon: Drink water and have two or three cups of black coffee.

Noon – 5 PM: Drink water if hungry but stop drinking coffee.

5PM: Have targeted amount of calories based on schedule, less 200 calories to account for the consumption of the protein shake at 9PM.

6PM: Have one coffee and go to the gym.

9PM: Have a protein shake and a snack if below your daily caloric intake goal.

10:30PM – 6:30 AM: Get lots of sleep.

This schedule can be an easy way to diet while not actively having to think about "starving" yourself to lose weight. Filling yourself in the morning and afternoon with water and coffee actually works to stave off any feeling of hunger whilst also getting a large fulfilling meal each day. It should be noted the above schedule is much more rigid than it needs to be. If you are interested in intermittent fasting, typically all you would have to do is not eat for at least six hours after waking up.

Ultimately, fasting is only recommended if your body can handle manipulating your insulin levels. That being said, the average healthy body was created with survival in mind and should be able to withstand eating once every 12-20 hours. 3000 years ago, the average person did not have a place on every corner where they could pull up and eat anything whenever they wanted.

Additional Perks of Intermittent Fasting:

- Intermittent fasting allows for large, fulfilling meals while on a diet. This means that after the initial shift to a caloric deficit, you are less likely to view the fasting as a diet, so you won't constantly be thinking about food.

- You don't have to plan and pack 3-5 meals a day, especially when trying to eat more for maintenance or for gaining muscle. Typically all I have done when I feel my body fat percentage is low enough is add in a protein shake or two per day during periods where I want to gain muscle and make sure my weight is increasing at a low controlled pace.

- There is no proven link to 16 hour fasting putting your body into <u>more</u> of a "survival mode," reducing your metabolism, <u>assuming the same overall daily caloric intake</u> vs. a comparable 3,4,5 meals a day diet.

- This diet strategy saves money & time. It is much easier on your time and budget to eat one big meal than 5 or 6 small ones. Thus this strategy does align with the <u>Wealth Pillar</u>.

- Intermittent fasting makes it easier to keep track of your calories. Your brain will, tactfully, underestimate how much you are eating. It is much easier to track one big meal each day than 6 smaller ones. Therefore, intermittent fasting lends itself to the calorie counting strategy, which is a foolproof way to ensure you are putting your body in a caloric deficit.

- Due to all the water you drink throughout the day to make you feel full generally you also hit the Institute of Medicine's recommendation for water intake. For the record the recommended water intake, as written by the Institute of Medicine, for a male is approximately 3.7 liters or 125 ounces daily. Given how much your body relies on H_2O as a catalyst and/or unit of transport for a variety of functions, a high water intake is always recommended. The majority of the human body is composed of water for a reason.

- Finally, the extra water intake helps facilitate the extra creatine and protein that will pass through your kidneys. These supplements are composed of bigger molecules which your body has a tougher time excreting.

What you put into your body does matter. A good diet is not temporary. It is life altering. However, society often views diets as temporary. The typical "Are you still on a diet?" remark itself implies a short term view. Reframe a diet as a long term commitment to your body. Just like a relationship, be loyal to it and it won't fail you.

H2 Exercise and Working out

Irrespective of your goal, be it losing body weight or gaining muscle, it is highly recommended you start lifting weights. During a diet the act of working out will assist in telling your body you need your muscle because of the stress you are putting on your muscles. The act of working out therefore, in theory, influences your body to elicit burning up fat storage instead of muscle storage. Additionally, sustaining a pound of muscle burns more calories than sustaining a pound of fat. It follow then that the more muscle you have as a percentage of your overall weight, the easier you will find it to lose additional weight. Conversely if you already have a lot of muscle the harder it will be to eat enough to sustain that muscle.

Regarding hormones, fat cells can secrete additional estrogen. Estrogen is necessary for all humans, but is generally thought of as the "female" hormone. Although estrogen is necessary in men, as it regulates a healthy libido and improves brain function, when estrogen levels become too high testosterone levels are reduced. Meaning a 200 pound male at 12% body fat is likely going to have a materially higher testosterone level than a 200 pound male at 35% body fat. Reduced testosterone levels have shown to negatively affect physical, sexual and emotional aspects of your life. Decreasing your body weight percent just low enough to show abdominals is a sure way to make the endocrine (hormone) system work for you instead of against you. If you have to pick between losing weight or building muscle it is recommended you lose weight first (to your targeted a body fat percentage) and only then make the shift in focus to building muscle.

Prioritizing your focus on lowering your body fat percentage before shifting your focus to gaining muscle is important as having a higher testosterone level influences muscle development & maintenance. Low testosterone directly influences the Social Pillar and can lead to feelings of sadness, depression and a decrease in self-confidence. Recall the Law of State Transference (S1.5) and that bringing any of these emotions into your conversation would likely end any social interaction before it starts. Furthermore, regarding the social implications and in particular dating, low levels of testosterone reduces your desire for sex, and without that primal motivation you are less likely to approach a woman you happen to find attractive. Let the endocrine system work for you instead of against you in your interactions with the opposite sex.

H2.1 Diet for Working Out

Assuming you finally hit your dieting goals and have a body fat percentage you are happy with, it is time to start focusing on building muscle. First and foremost make sure you don't make any drastic lifestyle changes. You have to gain muscle just as and if not more strategically than it took to lose fat. If you just start eating whatever you want you will find yourself spinning your wheels in an endless bulk/cut cycle. Instead, it is suggested to slowly start increasing your protein intake. This increase in consumption should help move your body from a deficit into at least maintenance. For example, if you were eating less than 1 gram of protein per body weight a day, then try to eat 1.2 grams of protein per pound of body weight a day. Calculate how many additional calories that would be every day. Would this incremental increase put you over your maintenance level? Are you now eating too much? How can you tell if this increase in consumption will actually help you build muscle instead of gaining fat?

The short answer is you can't. You are discovering a new baseline calorie level, and everyone's maintenance level will be different. The key here is to monitor this transition into a caloric surplus as closely as you can. Keep on tracking your weight and waist measurements. Use those abdominals as a visual barometer and "failsafe" to determine your probable body fat percentage composition. Using these indicators will provide you with a bench mark you can keep comparing yourself to each day, week and month.

So how can you tell if you are eating too much now with the shift in focus from losing weight to muscle growth?

The rate at which you can build muscle is contingent on how much muscle you already have. That is, there are diminishing returns to muscle growth. This means you could put on 10-20 pounds of muscle in your first year, but less in each subsequent year after that.

Enclosed below is a chart that you can use to determine if you are over eating for muscle gain.

Category	Max Rate of Muscle Growth per Month
Beginner (Low amount of existing muscle):	1.1-1.5% Growth of Lean Body Mass
Intermediate (5'10, 170 pounds 12% BF)*	0.4%-1% Growth of Lean Body Mass
Advanced (5'10, 180 pounds 10% BF)*	0.2%-0.35% Growth of Lean Body Mass

*These categories are subjective and the specific bodyweight composition examples given should be taken with a grain of salt.

This chart provides a rough estimate of the maximum muscle gain you can achieve per month. It is based on Alan Aragorn's chart from his book "Girth Control", which I found my personal success is most in line with. Remember, like all the weight tables, these are estimated numbers based on numerous assumptions, everyone is different. If you're interested in learning more about determining the estimated rate of muscle growth, I highly suggest Alan's book, "Girth Control".

So how is this max muscle growth chart useful??

This chart serves to assist in calculating how much muscle growth you could expect in terms of weight per month. For example, if you were a beginner and your weight increased by more than 1.5% of lean body mass in a month then it follows that you are likely over eating. Lean body mass is defined as your weight with no fat. If you weighed 180 pounds at 15% body fat then:

Lean Body Mass = (180)*(1-0.15) = 153 lbs

Back in section H1.2, Determining Body Fat Percentage, we went over how to ascertain a rough estimate of your body fat percentage. Combine the waist measurement target chart in section H1.2 to convert your waist measurement to an approximate estimate of your body fat percentage.

For example:

Waist: 29.9"
Height: 5'10
Weight: 148 lbs

Based on this information and the table in H1.2, your body fat percentage would be 10-12%. Let's assume 11% (average of 10-12%)

Therefore,

Approximate Lean Body Mass: 148 x (1-0.11) = 131.72 lbs

Given in this example the weight of 148 lbs and a height of 5'10, you would probably fall under the beginner category of the "Girth Control" chart. It follows then that:

Maximum Muscle Gain Per Month: 131.72 * 1.5% =1.98lbs

Therefore, if your weight on average increased much more than 1.98 pounds per month than you know that you are eating too much for your current lifestyle.

Logically then it follows that a "beginner" is likely to experience the most growth in muscle. The trade-off however, is that it will be more difficult to ascertain if the weight you are putting on is from fat or muscle. Alternatively, an advanced weightlifter would be able to tell if he put on too much fat.

For example, from the table:

Advanced Lifter

Weight: 180lbs
Body Fat Percentage: 10%
Lean Body Mass: 180 * (1-0.10) = 162 lbs
Max Muscle Gain Per Month: 162 * 0.2% = 0.32 lbs

Therefore, if the advanced lifter gains a pound in a month the individual can assume that the bulk of that weight gain was fat.

To summarize, beginners can put on muscle weight faster but will have a tougher time determining if that weight was from fat or from muscle so make sure as a beginner you are using waist measurements and abdominals as an additional indicator of your body fat percentage level. Too many people diet and then put the weight all back on. Don't be another victim to the endless cut and bulk cycle.

H2.2 Transition in Focus from Dieting to Muscle Gain

Recall the diet itself did not alter dramatically from the caloric deficit phase. We are still intermittent fasting but have upped the calories during the non-fasting window to ensure our body is no longer in a catabolic state. Specifically, initial extra calories when transitioning from fat loss focus to muscle gain focus should be in the form of eating more whey protein. Protein is made up of amino acids and without these amino acids it would be impossible to build, mend, or even preserve muscle tissue. During this shift in focus it is recommended to increase your protein intake one scoop before and one scoop after your workout. These additional two scoops of protein each day, mixed with water, will probably increase your daily caloric intake by about 360 calories (contingent on your specific protein product). This increase alone is likely to turn your body back into a surplus, as 2 additional scoops each day increases your weekly caloric intake by almost 2500. Near the end of my dieting phase, I was losing on average 0.6 pounds a week and we now know a pound of fat has approximately 3500 calories. Assuming the weight I lost was mostly fat, it goes to follow that:

Weight loss per week: 0.6lbs

1 lbs of fat: 3500 calories

Average Caloric Deficit per week: 3500 * 0.6 = 2100 calories

Consequently, I knew these additional two scoops a day of protein at 2500 calories per week were likely going to bring me back to caloric maintenance or preferably slightly over. However, I still utilized the maximum muscle gain chart in H2.1 to ensure my weight was increasing at a level aligned with max muscle gain. This is critical in determining how many extra calories you can get away with each week during this transitional shift in focus. Ultimately, if the scale isn't increasing after switching to a muscle gain focus, despite increasing your protein intake, it can be beneficial to have a day (usually leg or back day) where you should eat a bit more (300-1000 calories) to make sure your weight stops dropping at the very least. These additional calories you in take when the scale isn't going up should be viewed as a treat. If you start to gaining weight too quickly after this small weekly treat then you can ascertain causation and know that without the treat you are likely eating close/slightly above maintenance. Again, remember this is all based on my own experience, but it does indicate how methodical one should be when attempting to establish a new baseline for muscle growth.

H2.3 Set Weightlifting Goals

Like painting, most of the work for lifting weight is actually in the preparation work. This is why progress measurement and dieting comes before workout routines in this book. Just like when setting weight targets and waist measurement goals for dieting, in weight lifting you also should have goals to strive for. These goals need to be things you can quantifiably measure. A simple goal is the popular Adonis Golden ratio where you take your waist measurement and multiply it by 1.618 to find a targeted shoulder measurement. This is the "proposed" ratio for men that makes their body overall attractive. Frame this measurement as the male counterpart to the female "hourglass" shape. For example:

Waist: 32"
Adonis Golden Ratio: 32x 1.618 = 51.78"

This means your shoulder width target is 51.78", so if your shoulders are only at 50 inches you should either work on losing fat on your waist or start hitting those lateral raises. For the record it will likely be much easier to hit that waist.

You should always strive to be constantly improving and the gym is a way to physically see your progress. Not only that but you also get positive visual feedback from others and from the mirror which increases your overall confidence level. This increase in confidence and increased perception of your own self-worth will translate into hopefully finding a life partner you are genuinely attracted to and not just "settling" for whomever happens to be around you at any given time.

There are two types of targets you should aim for when working out:

1.) Absolute Strength Targets
2.) Relative Strength Targets

Absolute Strength Targets:

- 315 lbs Deadlift

- 280 lbs Squat

- 200 lbs Bench Press

These goals are there to guide your overall strength and are arbitrary. Set absolute goals based on where you are at now. Absolute strength is a reflection of how much you can lift regardless of your body weight. This means that you can be absolutely strong but still look unaesthetically pleasing. That being said, absolute strength targets should be used to guide your progress and help to align your personal goals to that of societies. This makes your workout goals relatable to other people's work out goals despite everyone's different body types and compositions. Finally, using absolute strength goals is a good way to build a sense of community in your gym.

Relative Strength Targets:

Relative strength targets are a bit more important as they take into account your approximate body weight or composition. Below are some more complex weight lifting targets I suggest you strive for and ensure you keep progressing. These relative strength targets are a good way to benchmark yourself against the previous versions of you. It also helps to illustrate who is stronger if you do decide to have a gym partner or two. Not to put yourself above others, but rather to introduce a natural competitive nature that in the modern world just does not easily exist. In society today, everyone gets a participation ribbon just for showing up. Competition with colleagues in the gym is a good way to push yourselves to greater feats of strength as you can utilize the natural ego that you never want your good friends to beat you. This is one of the few times an ego can actually help you, but remember that it is an ego. Cognitively knowing part of your competitive nature is fueled by ego stops giving it power. Instead of rejecting this ego you can use it with a smile knowing that it is the primary reason why you want to one-up your colleagues' personal bests. Below are some of the superior weightlifting relative strength targets:

Exercise (5 reps)	Very Fit	Intermediate	Advanced
Incline Bench Press	95% of Body Weight	120% body Weight	140% Body Weight
Weighted Chin Ups	30% Body Weight Added	40% Body Weight Added	65% Body Weight Added
Standing Shoulder Press	65% Body Weight	80% Body Weight	100% Body Weight
Bicep Curls	60% Body Weight	70% Body Weight	75% Body Weight

These relative strength goals are based off of Kinobody's Greg O'Gallaghers (Popular YouTube Persona) strength goals and adjusted slightly based on personal experience and other various readings. Hitting these goals will not just indicate strength and give you a goal to strive for, but also are indicative of specific aesthetic body images. Paraphrasing slightly, Greg O'Gallagher states that achieving typically the very fit column targets would look like Brad Pitt in "Fight Club", the intermediate would be a more filled out version of Brad Pitt in "Troy", and finally the advanced column would look something more like Chris Evans as Captain America.

Tracking your weightlifting progress is extremely important for quantifying your progress; however, it is suggested to only track certain key compound lifts with a pen and paper or else you can lose sight on what lifts are most important. The key exercises to track of are your bench press, squat and deadlift progression. Tracking the four listed relative strength exercises is also a good way to determine how close you are to certain body images. Most other isolated exercises will improve naturally as your strength increases in the compound movement lifts. Moreover, the compound movement lifts allow your body to move in the way that it is designed, allowing one to be more functionally strong in everyday life. Exercises that use more than one muscle simultaneously teach the muscles to work together like they would in more day-to-day circumstances and can create a more overall athletic appearance.

H2.4 Workout routines

This section is comprised of a rough outline of what a typical workout routine could look like. Please see Appendix 6 for a concise summarized table. It is proposed to use this routine as a simple template to generate ideas from but remember to tailor it to your own body's needs. Typically the core of each workout should be a compound movement with a general focus on a different targeted muscle group each day.

Sunday – Legs

Monday – Shoulder

Tuesday – Bicep

Wednesday – Chest

Thursday - Tricep

Friday – Back

Saturday – Core and/or targeted muscle group or rest

Notice the major muscle groups legs, back and chest are spread out throughout the week as these heavier lifts tend to more easily fatigue the central nervous system (CNS). Spreading them out allows the CNS ample time to recover.

Saturday, as illustrated above, does state core and/or targeted muscle group. Saturday serves as a catch all day to focus on something you feel is lacking.

Below are five exercises for each muscle group that I found myself carrying out most often. Everyone is different so don't religiously follow this workout plan. Think of it as a blueprint. Simply use my schedule and list of exercises as a template and switch around items you don't want with exercises you do want. These lists are numbered according to how I normally carried out my workouts; starting with exercise # 1 and working your way down. It is recommended to switch up the order or cycle in new secondary exercises once a month to assist in shocking the body. If unsure what a specific exercise is or how to perform said exercise correctly consider looking up the YouTube content of Jeff Cavalier from Athlean X. Jeff's physical therapy background is a competitive advantage that I find most other fitness YouTube provider's lack. A link to his channel is provided on Appendix #12

Sunday – Legs Exercise Schedule

1. Barbell Squat (Track Progress)

2. Leg Press

3. Seated Leg Curl (Hamstring)

4. Seated Leg Extension

5. Standing Calf Raise

Note, you can cycle out exercise # 3-5 with other leg exercises once a month to help shock the muscle. Additional leg exercises could include, but are not limited to, walking dumbbell lunges, goblet squats & even Romanian deadlifts. It is generally best to start with the squat as this is the exercise to gauge progress every week. Regarding the leg press, it is best to determine what muscle you want to focus on. Putting your feet higher up on the pad will better target your hamstrings and glutes and put your body at a mechanical disadvantage (meaning you will lift less than what your quads can do if your feet are placed more naturally).

Monday – Shoulder Exercise Schedule

1. Standing Shoulder Press (Track Progress)

2. Military Press (Track Progress)

3. Bent-Over Rear Delt Raise

4. Lateral Raise

5. Reverse Machine Fly

Consider cycling out exercise # 3-5 with other shoulder exercises monthly to help keep the muscle guessing. Additional shoulder exercises could include, but are not limited to, seated shoulder press, front raises & the upright row. Contemplate switching between the standing shoulder press and the military press every month to better gauge progress on both lifts. Ultimately, whichever exercise you select to do second you will be weaker in. The main reason why standing shoulder press is proposed over seated shoulder press is standing exercises generally activate your core as well. This is why standing shoulder press is included in the relative strength chart exercise and seated shoulder press is not. If you are not used to performing the standing shoulder press I propose you do a lighter weight until you can better engage your core to balance the weight. Most books are hesitant to recommend the standing shoulder press as there is more room for injury and error.

Two of the 5 exercises on the shoulder day list focus on rear delts. This is mainly because of personal preference caused by a belief that my rear delts don't get hit very often by any other exercises on any other day. I found rear delt targeting helped better my overall body posture as I work in front of a computer at least 9 hours a day. From a social perspective, this improvement in posture helps you carry yourself better and displays a more prominent degree of openness and natural self-confidence. People are much more likely to approach you, ask you for help and enjoy being around you if you aren't closing yourself off to the world subconsciously by expressing poor body language. Consider becoming more rear delt focused on shoulder day if you occasionally find yourself hunched or slouched forward. Chances are if you have an office job your body posture is suffering, so take some action and change it for the better while working out. Do these rear delt exercises not only for the social aspect, but also to lessen the risk of back & shoulder injury.

Finally, side delt focus is proposed if your body posture is okay and you are striving to achieve the Adonis Golden Ratio. However, targeting these lateral delts is not the primary driver to achieve the Adonis ratio, instead it is a lower waist measurement via dieting and proper nutrition. Front delts generally get hit enough during chest day, but front raises are an excellent way to target them if you want to focus on bigger front delts.

Tuesday – Bicep Exercise Schedule

1.   Weighted Chin Up (Track Progress)

2.   Ez Curl Bar Bicep Curl (Track Progress)

3.   Overhead Cable Curl

4.   Preacher Curl

5.   Incline Hammer Curls

Weighted chin ups might seem odd to do on bicep day, but chin ups can rely heavily on biceps once the back starts fatiguing; additionally biceps were purposely put on Tuesday to ensure they are recovered for back day come Friday. Other bicep exercises could include but are not limited to standard barbell curl, concentration curl & the Zottman curl. Bicep days are also a good day to throw in exercises that recruit your forearm and wrist. Grip strength and forearm strength are important factors in increasing your overall lifting potential, especially for deadlifting. Consider supinating your arms on the way up whenever you are doing a curl exercise that allows for it. Bicep

Tuesday's are also days where one can fit in an additional ab/core exercise at the end of the routine.

Wednesday – Chest Exercise Schedule

1. Barbell Bench Press (Track Progress)

2. Push Ups

3. Peck Deck Machine

4. Seated Machine Chest Press

5. Low Cable Cross Over

Consider cycling out exercise # 3-5 with other chest exercises monthly to ensure the muscle is still being surprised. The bench press is probably the most sought out lift and the one that is more likely to be used in comparisons when relating yourself to other people. Don't fall prey to societal norms and compare yourself to other people. Instead benchmark yourself only to your previous self. The goal in the gym is constant progress, not being better than someone else. If the bench press is an absolute indicator of strength, push ups are an indicator of overall fitness and body composition. If you can push around a lot of weight on the bench press but can't do a single push up chances are you have a high body fat percentage. Another challenge you can do is attempting to do 100 push ups in an allotted time period and then trying to do better than your previous timed record every week. This way you are still progressing, but instead of more weight on the bar it is a race against time. Can you do 100 push ups in 7, 6, 5 or 4 minutes? Since barbell bench press and push ups both utilize your shoulders for stability, exercises # 3-5 attempt to take stability, and therein front delts, out of the equation. Additional chest exercises could include, but are not limited to, dumbbell bench press, decline bench press and weighted chest dips.

<u>Thursday – Tricep Exercise Schedule</u>

1. Weighted Triceps Dip

2. Cable push-down

3. Skullcrushers

4. Seated overhead dumbbell extension

5. Close-Grip Bench Press

Since triceps day is after chest day (in my schedule), there is no progress to physically write down today. Your chest will be fatigued from the day before, so finishing with a light weight high rep close-grip bench press after tiring out your triceps will compromise your pushing ability. Triceps are 2/3's of your arm, so make sure you put in the extra work. Before you knock cable push-downs, as per Boeckh-Behrens and Buskies in "Fitness Strength Training: The Best Exercises and Methods of Sport and Health", "this exercise activates the lateral head of the triceps greater than skull crushers…or any other major triceps exercise".

<u>Friday – Back Exercise Schedule</u>

1. Barbell Deadlift (Track Progress)

2. Wide-Grip Pull up (Weighted preferable)

3. Bent-Over Barbell Row

4. Wide-Grip Seated Cable Row

5. Standing T-Bar Row

Consider cycling out exercise # 3-5 with other back exercises monthly. Back day, at least in my experience, is the most draining on the central nervous system. The proper deadlift form utilizes all major parts of your entire body and is the most indicative exercise for overall strength. The primary reason why Saturday is a bit of a catch all and rest day is because it is expected that one will go all out Friday night at the gym and leave nothing on the table.

Saturday – Focus and Rest Day

Typically this is the day where you should focus on working out a part of your body that you feel is lagging or hampering your progress on your tracked lifts. Contingent on a successful Friday workout, you might want to take the day off.

As mentioned, this schedule can be found on Appendix 6 in a more accessible format. Tailor this schedule to your life at your own discretion. Frame the schedule as a proposed base to start with and customize it according to your own goals. Six days out of seven at the gym for 45 minutes to an hour may not be possible for some so you may need to organize your gym days into push and pull days. That is, doing back and biceps one day and chest and triceps the other. Ultimately, if you are paying for a gym membership, consider at least heading to the gym three days a week so you can get in a good leg day, push day and pull day each week.

It is not just about the exercises you do. The primary goal is to shock the muscle so that it needs to repair itself and force the body to adapt to the stressor. If a certain exercise makes you uncomfortable or gives any kind of joint pain then drop the exercise and hit the muscle from another angle. Don't injure yourself. You are the only one who knows what your body is truly capable of. To add to the list of never-ending disclaimers, I am not a doctor or a personal trainer. If you are interested in personalizing a workout schedule for yourself, you could take the schedule in Appendix 6 and bring it to your personal trainer. This will, in effect, take a base generic blueprint and customize it to your own overall health and fitness goals.

H2.5 – Lift Heavy vs. High Reps

Now this subject has a bit of controversy behind it which means this book has to touch on it.

There is some research that suggests that certain muscle fibers respond better to certain types of training. Slow twitch muscle fibers work well for endurance (high rep) activities whereas fast twitch muscle fibers work well for explosive training (heavy lifting). The theory is, if your body generally does above average during events like long distance running relative to someone of a similar fitness level then it's likely you have a greater percent of your muscle labeled as slow twitch muscle fibers.

Basically, the main understanding is if you think your body has slower twitch muscle fibers then you are better off doing exercises with higher reps that favor that type of activity to ensure more muscle fibers are firing and tiring out for hypertrophy to occur.

Alternatively, others may react better to lifting heavier weights with less reps. Lifting heavier aligns with fast twitch muscle fibers. Looking around the gym, generally you will notice bigger guys lift bigger weights, but what you can't prove in hindsight is if they achieved that physique with more reps or with more weight. Obviously not all of us are the same, and many of us, myself included, cannot easily tell what our bodies will respond to unless you take action. With that in mind, I believe the Average Joe would benefit more by lifting heavier.

Lift heavier. Not because of the muscle fiber, but because of our brain. Assuming you don't know what type of training you respond to better, than reframe the lift heavy vs. more reps conundrum in its entirety. Frame it so you know you will want that last rep more at 200 lbs on the bench than you will at 135 lbs, assuming the same total amount of weight pressed. Reinforce this frame by logically considering each rep automatically becomes more important when there are less of them total. The brain is more likely to give up on the light weight 12th rep of the fourth set (48th rep) than it is on the heavy weight 5th rep of the fourth set (20th rep) assuming total volume equal. This believe will enable you to work more intensely when the weight is heavier. The "one more rep" mantra will be more significant for you. You will push yourself harder for that last rep. This increase in intensity will fuel your results.

As an additive perk, a smaller rep range allows for more incremental small weight increases. An extra 5 pounds at 20 reps is only 100 more pounds in volume total. However, 5 pounds at 48 reps is 240 more pounds in volume. Therefore it is actually easier to incrementally increase the weight when lifting heavy. This small incremental weight increase is highly motivating, allowing you to reflect on your achievements more often and provide more meaningful genuine excitement when achieving personal bests. These small incremental weight increases can further be framed as a visual indicator of your own constant self-improvement. It follow then that lifting heavier weights in the long run is naturally more motivating.

Lifting heavier, as recommended above, is not for everyone. Visibly the term "heavy" is a relative term, so make it relative to you. Don't lift heavy if your body can't take it. Lifting heavy does not mean lifting unsafe. Know your capabilities. Know them by taking action safely through your own experiences.

H3 Social Benefits of Exercise

There are many social benefits of exercise; however, don't go to the gym to hit on girls. Do go to the gym to work out. Utilize the gym as a tool to transition from your work life into your social life. It is strongly advised to go to a gym as opposed to working out at home. At the gym you surround yourself with people who are actively improving themselves... just like you. Additionally the gym membership is a commitment. It means you are serious about working out and an admission to yourself that you are serious about improving yourself. The act of going to a gym can be motivating in of itself and also sets a base for support if you start veering off your weight loss or muscle gain plan. Before you go out on the town to meet people on a Friday night, head to the gym. Say "hi" to the people working when you walk in and start shaking off the cobwebs from the daily work monotony. Heading to the gym with a partner is also a great way to get you in a social mood and get in the mindset for a fun evening. This will help create social momentum or at least start the ball rolling to getting out there and meet new people.

As already mentioned, a lower body fat percentage correlates itself to higher testosterone levels. This will mean you will be more interested in the opposite sex. The more genuinely interested you are in someone the more they are to be interested in you. This is a primary principle in carrying out engaging conversation (S1.4) and most important it is critical when attempting to achieve meaningful relationships. Higher testosterone translates into a higher sex drive. This means you will be even more naturally congruent (S1.3) and genuine when expressing your interest/attraction. Finally, a more self-confident, overall happier you will transcend to your potential partner via the Law of State Transference (S1.5). The bottom line is, a higher testosterone level lends itself favorably into three of the ten Core Social competencies.

The three pillars of self-improvement are not mutually exclusive. A healthy person brings that healthy lifestyle into all aspects of their lives, including their dating life. The proposed dieting and workout goals in this book serve as a loose framework to physically build a better self. It is proposed to take certain parts of this Health section and tailor it to your own life. As long as you go to the gym consistently, with intensity, and start tracking your progress you will start seeing results. A woman will not care about how much you bench, but she will care that you can take care of yourself. Working out is one of the highest forms of self-respect and is a visual indicator of your constant belief in self-improvement. Make sure you work out for yourself and not just for attracting a lady or for any type of other external validation. This will ensure you are working out for the long term and teach you to motivate yourself from within. Finally, working out reduces the risk of many diseases, reduces stress, depression and anxiety, forces you to get out of the house, improves sexual performance and restores libido. It is no surprise that these perks inevitability give your self-image and self-confidence a boost which you can than carry into your dating life both physically and emotionally.

At the end of the day, nothing is more important than your health. Take action, start lifting, and start visually progressing.

PILLAR #3: WEALTH

Now for the dry part... **Wealth...**

However dry the material is, as one of the most exciting Chartered Professional Accountants known today (low bar I know), I will attempt to make this topic interesting.

Any man who can't handle money lets money handle him. This means your integrity can be compromised for something material. Much like a man can be a slave to smoking, so to can money chain you. In fact, money can be just as perverse to your veracity and even more subtle all the same. Exciting, right?

For many people this section will act to set the stage for ensuring success in the other two pillars. Moreover, one should know by now that these three pillars of Wealth, Health and Social all directly interrelate with each other.

Money itself should be viewed as a tool. Money opens doors. Money motivates people. Money allows you to focus on self-actualization after basic needs are met and enables one to live a healthier lifestyle. Money alone, however, will not make you happy or even healthy and has marginally decreasing returns on happiness as ones bank account grows. That is to say, the amount of money one makes on a dollar per dollar basis can still manage to increase "happiness" but it does so at a decreasing rate.

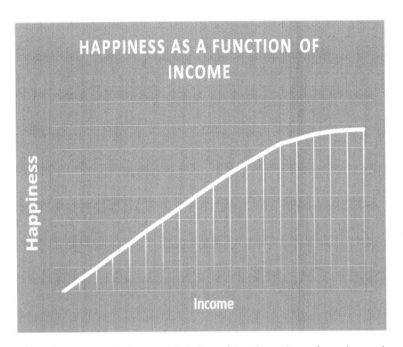

The above graph is completely subjective given happiness is something not readily quantifiable and thus has different thresholds for everyone; however, most rational people would agree money is more meaningful when basic needs are not being met. If basic needs are not being met one could not hope to efficiently eat healthier, constantly grow as an individual, and plan out their life for the future. One does not easily prepare for the future when one is constantly struggling just to get by.

Illustrated below is the famous Maslow's Hierarchy of Needs originally proposed by Abraham Maslow in the 1943 paper "A Theory of Human Motivation." The credit for the image is due to simplypsychology.org. The pyramid correlates well with the theory that happiness as a function of money increases at a decreasing rate:

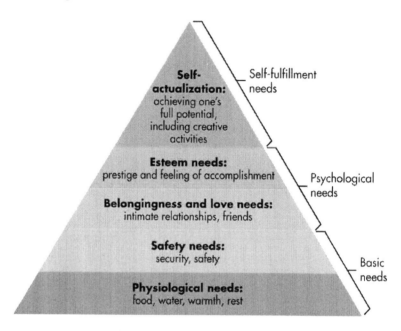

Being in a survival setting focuses on the present, how could you hope to be the best you can be if you are constantly worried about putting food on the table or keeping a roof over your head? Interestingly, you will note in the social section of this book that being present is a good thing for dating. The fact that you are thinking about your future or money in general actually makes you less cognitively present to your current environment. That's why accountants like me, or other stereotypical jobs you associate with introversion (looking at you engineering) can have an immensely more difficult time being in the moment and relating to people. This introversion can be readily apparent when contrasted against say a high school dropout who is a club promoter but gets tons of ladies. He gets lots of women because he is "fun", lives in the moment and doesn't take himself too seriously. Furthermore, the club promoter career is congruent with that identity because that's who he really is and he really may not care (at least at that time) about his future. The average reader of this book is likely more "well-off" than just scraping by and is probably more introverted then the standard club promoter which means it is much more likely that you struggle with keeping present more so than you struggle thinking about your future. I mean if you have disposable income for a self-help book then you are obviously on the right track in life. So how do you focus on the Social and Health Pillars without being inhibited by a lack of money? This section will be composed of two main sections: Savings and Investments.

W1: Savings

Much like how you would measure progress in the Health Pillar (how much you can lift, how much you weigh and even your waist size) you can also measure your relative success at savings. Like the scale, cash doesn't lie. Credit can, but cash does not.

In order to measure financial progress you first have to create a benchmark. Start with taking action. Look at your bank account history over the past twelve months. Where did it start at and where is it now? Take the current balance, less the beginning balance 12 months ago, and divide that number by the beginning balance. For example:

Starting Bank Balance: $12,000
Current Bank Balance: $15,000
Bank Account Growth Rate: ($15,000-$12000)/$12000 = 25%

You can use this percent as a hard goal for what you want next year. Be aware that since the goal is based on a growth rate, the higher the growth rate the harder it is to sustain. This historical analysis will easily enable you to see if you are spending more than you are bringing in. If your bank account went down year over year you have to ask yourself the hard questions, "What can I cut back on?" Or "Have I lived beyond my means?" Set a goal of how much money you want in your bank account by the end of next year based on your expectations, using your historical growth rate as an indicative, ballpark figure of what is reasonable.

Say in my example above I want $20,000 in my bank account by next year, which is 33% more than what I have currently. This is higher than the amount saved last year as we are planning to save $5,000 as opposed to the $3,000 we previously achieved, so how am I planning to accomplish this feat? What is going to change? What is my plan of action?

Should one take an additional job to increase income? Money on the side can be a good thing but it has a few key trade-offs, mainly time & energy. As mentioned at the very beginning of this book people today already spend the bulk of their time awake generating money as opposed to socializing, being healthy and quite simply just taking care of themselves and living life.

In my case, last year I worked at a tax institution as a "tax professional" during the tax season for some extra money. Now without the side job, my basic needs were already met so why did I do it? I wanted to start meeting new people and try to help them save money on taxes. This actually left me in a more talkative state for going out and meeting more people. Most importantly, I did genuinely like trying to help people with their money issues. Nothing made me happier than seeing someone's eyes light up when I could tell them that by doing slightly different would save them a couple hundred dollars next year. This type of work allowed for a degree of social momentum to build naturally and thus combined my Wealth and Social goals. However, this brilliant idea soon backfired as working fulltime in my normal job, with this tax institution side job, while studying and writing this book soon left me not wanting to go out at all. Even when I did manage to go out I could barely be present enough to engage with people and attempting to come in at a higher energy level than the people I was approaching was an arduous task.

Conversely, another side job I did was delivering papers on the side. While smaller in side income relative to the income from the tax institution, a paper route forced me to be physically active on the days I wasn't at the gym. The paper route was only 3 hours a week instead of working 20 hours as a "tax pro". Not only did this paper route increase my income but it also aligned with the Health Pillar and left me feeling good afterwards without "taxing" my ability to socialize with others. It also brought me closer to the body type I was aiming for, going from 190 to 160 lbs while increasing my income by $100-150 a month.

Ultimately, while one side job allowed for me to be in a talkative state, the other was actually better at increasing my overall mood which I brought into all my social interactions, dating or otherwise. Therefore in this specific case I would choose the newspaper route over the "tax pro" job, as I didn't need the additional side income as much as I needed the Health and Social aspects of my life. There will always be a trade off in the ways you allocate your time so make sure you are cognitive about how much time you are spending on each of the three pillars, assuming you make enough money to cover the first two layers of Maslow's Hierarchy of Needs (Basic needs & Safety). Often when the actions you take relate to multiple pillars it generally correlates with you more efficiently utilizing your time to improve yourself.

Main jobs and side jobs are just the start of how to get your bank account growing. Far more important is what you do with your hard earned money. Ever hear, "It's not what you make, it's what you save"? Savings is driven by income and expenses, but people have much more direct influence on their expenses than their income. It follows then that in order to hit your savings goals you need to be disciplined in your expenditures.

How to be disciplined in a land full of comforts?

Consumerism is rampant and all around you, attempting to trick you into buying things you don't need with credit you don't have. Should you give in to the instant gratification trend or will you learn to value something more simply because you put more time and effort in to get it? Remember, if something is easy then chances are it will have no real long lasting value to you. Patiently saving and paying for that one trip, in cash, you always wanted to go on will make you appreciate and value that trip much more than putting it on the credit card. Plus, then you won't have to worry about how you will pay for it when you get back. You will, in effect, get more out of that trip by saving for it ahead of time. Saving for it implies more appreciation when you are there. If already in a relationship, setting a goal for a trip will align both of your agendas. Combat "wanton" consumerism by memorizing the wise words of the band U2... "What you don't have you don't need it now" from the song "Beautiful Day". An individual should be able to rely on his or her own resourcefulness to get by. Anything you need immediately has power over you and anything that has power over you limits you and makes you internally stagnated. By extension to the Social Pillar, it can be argued that anything material that has power over you can make you unattractive as you are not the true driving force behind your actions.

So how do you cut expenditures and master your finances?

First, cut out the things in your life that cost money and make you unhealthy or unmotivated. This again aligns your Wealth goals with that of your Social and Health ones. For example, cut out smoking if you are still smoking. (Easier said than done). In today's day and age you are probably seen as unattractive to the type of women you probably want to attract. Not for the obvious superficial reasons like that smoky lingering smell, but for the fact you need something external that doesn't come from yourself. A man's energy comes from within. The fact that someone could have power over your emotions just by taking your smokes away for a week displays an internal weakness and neediness that is hard to come back from. In addition, smoking would affect how much you could run, lift, reduces your stamina in the bedroom as well as hits your bank account.

Really, smoking is an anti-symbol of what this book stands for as it goes against all three pillars.

Liquor serves as another easier place to start cutting. Booze is discretional, costs money and in excess, is detrimental against your Health and Social abilities. While some booze has been seen to be good for your health it is not healthy when you drink more than moderation and end up binging at your local fast food joint at 2 o'clock in the morning. Even worse, if you drink too much and end up hungover in the morning you miss valuable time you could be doing something productive. Liquor is a crutch in a social setting; as mentioned in the Social section, this liquid courage means you could come to rely on alcohol to be confident when approaching a woman you like. Relying on anything external that doesn't come from yourself should be seen as an internal weakness and is probably incongruent with your actual personality when you are sober. Liquor is an iconic example of situational confidence. You don't need a shot to go up and tell a woman you like her. All you need to do is admit you are scared and go and do it anyway.

Second, further cut back on anything you determine is discretional. Focus on cutting other unhealthy habits you have and reflect on why you do them. Is it just to relax? Is there something stressing in your life that you need to use this habit to unwind? Whatever is the stressor causing this habit is what you need to figure out and attack as that's the ground zero source of the problem. Take life in your own hands and don't run away or self-medicate from your problems. You will actually find taking action, even if you are not sure of what the outcome will be, is better than being fearful and doing nothing. If you are addicted to video games, gambling or smoking don't be too proud to seek help. Addictions inherently take more than they give. You can't be a Sun personality with an underlying addiction or dependency, at least not in the long run.

Now that we have gone through the basics of income generation and expense cutting, let's assume from our previous example we have a goal of savings of $5,000 this year. Last year, in the example, we saved $3,000. How will we come up with the additional $2,000 on top of that this year? To link to the above income generating and expense cutting paragraphs, I would start a newspaper route three hours a week and assume that drinking was costing me at least $20.00 a week.

Newspaper Router Income: $100 per month
Drinking Expenses: $20 per week
New Additional Savings: $100 + ($20*4 weeks) = $180 monthly
Annual Additional Savings: $180* 12 months = $2,160 annually

It is that simple. Not only did this solution allow us to achieve our $2,000 shortfall (assuming all else held constant) but it also aligns with our Health and Social goals. Moreover, once you have that extra money you could always reallocate some of it to help with Social and Health aspects of your life by buying healthier foods, being able to afford those monthly gym memberships, joining a social club, attending skill building workshops or just taking a lifestyle course like cooking.

Now let's make a safe assumption and assume in your case it's not so simple. Life has many curve balls and emergencies that arise seemingly out of nowhere and empty your hard earned savings. A key tool in saving money is setting a budget. Now don't roll your eyes. Budgets are a pivotal tool in determining company performance for owners, banks and management bonuses so why would they not matter in your personal life as well? Think of yourself as your own company. The only person who is accountable for its performance is you. You are the primary shareholder, controller, and CEO of your life. So how do you set a corporate budget up for yourself? The equations are simple:

Let "Take Home Income" = Revenue

So revenue equals the actual amount you see enter your bank account every pay period from your job. This simplifies your budget as it's now already taken out the standard tax and payroll deductions etc.

The next page is an example of a company budget plan for generic company "XYZ" and how it is used to identify issues using variance.

Income Statement

Company XYZ

Actual vs. Budgeted Variance Analysis

For the month of August 31, 2016

	Actual	Budgeted	Variance
Revenue	536,799	800,000	263,201
Cost of Sales	327,275	576,000	248,725
Gross Profit	209,524	224,000	14,476
Direct Expenses:			
Automotive and Travel	10,219	11,980	1,761
Meals	2,403	965	1,438
Telephone & Utilities	2,026	3,354	1,328
Salaries & Benefits	42,396	41,785	611
Shipping/Shop Supplies	151	5,805	5,654
Total Direct Expenses	57,195	63,888	6,693
Administrative Expenses			
Bad Debts	-	126	126
Bank Charges & Interest	462	804	342
Computer Prog/Maint	4,317	3,464	853
Insurance	5,278	5,266	12
Marketing	1,007	5,254	4,247
Office and Postage	1,457	3,000	1,543
Rent - Building	18,499	18,725	226
Repairs/Maintenance/Janitor	1,975	4,407	2,432
Total Admin Expenses	32,997	41,046	8,049
Income from Operations (EBITDA):	119,332	119,066	266
Other (Income) Expenses			
Interest Expense	4,645	8,253	3,608
Amortization	4,193	4,247	54
Gain/Loss Foreign Exchange	(15,317)	-	15,317
Total Other Income	(6,480)	12,500	18,980
Net Income	125,812	106,566	19,246

Luckily for us the details of the company income statement don't matter. However, like a successful company, you should go over your actual monthly spending performances and decide what you could do better. In company XYZ's case one would be able to quickly identify that the company sold less than expected but its direct and administrative expense variances were favorable... probably due to good management and cost cutting. The net result was in line with the budget with a small operating positive variance. You should also note that while the bottom line came in approximately $19,000 better than expected it is being driven by a non-recurring gain (foreign exchange gain). Make sure you are able to <u>distinguish between recurring expenses you incur, like groceries vs. "one off items" like vehicle repair</u>. This is vital. In your personal life you will always have non-recurring expenses that you will have to cover in order to achieve your financial goals. A proper budget should also incorporate cyclicality such as months where spending will be higher (I'm looking at you Christmas). You must create a buffer in all the other months in order to cover the perceived overspending you are likely to do around Christmas time. Creating an additional margin of safety to cover these non-recurring emergencies or seasonal spending is more than recommended, it is **required**. A budget needs to incorporate a potential "rainy day" savings plan.

So how do you create your own budget and compare actual results against it?

This is where you need to take some action. First look back over your past twelve monthly bank statements and identify what are the items you pay for each month that are beyond your immediate control to cut. Things like rent, utilities, food and gas...basically separate out anything that's essential for living (The floor levels of Maslow's Hierarchy of Needs). Any expenses incurred to earn the income you generate should also be separated out. Together, these expenses collectively make up the Non-Discretionary Spending section of your budget.

The next section is Discretionary Spending. This would include items like entertainment, gifts, shopping, cable and internet, parties and hobbies. Anything you have a habit of spending money on in the past that is likely to continue and if you didn't spend that money maybe your perceived "happiness" or standard of living would suffer, but you wouldn't "need it". This requires unbiased, objective judgement.

With the previous 12 month monthly bank statement information you can start building a monthly budget and measure how well you did against that said budget in any given month. Any spreadsheet or even a piece of paper will do. Recall in our example we need a "bottom line" to equal $5,000 annually. Or rather $416.67 a month. The desired monthly net income target of your personal budget should be whatever you want your annual savings to be divided by 12. Achieving this small task each month will enable you to gauge your progress and identify issues in the month it occurs before it becomes too late and you can't easily rectify the habitual increase in spending practice. Doing this each month will enable you to answer, "Where has my hard earned money gone?"

On the next page is a sample of how a typical personal budget could look and how it should be contrasted to actual results. Note how it is fairly similar to a corporate budget. The budget serves to help break down which expenses are Discretionary and which ones are Non-Discretionary.

Income Statement
Johnny "Charisma" Doe
Actual vs. Budgeted Variance Analysis
For the month of August 31, 2016

	Actual	Budgeted	Variance
Revenue	3,100	3,100	0
Non-Discretionary Spending			
Gas for Car	168	160	8
Meals	220	250	30
Utilities (Water, Sewage, Power)	350	400	50
Cell Phone	80	80	0
Rent	800	800	0
Vehicle Payment	106	106	0
Vehicle Insurance	120	120	0
Property Tax	200	200	0
Total Essential Spending	2,044	2,116	72
Total Income After Essentials	1,056	984	72
Discretionary Spending			
Going out meals	200	73	127
Gym membership	50	50	0
Smoking	0	0	0
Booze	0	0	0
Gifts for Friends/Shopping	80	20	60
Entertainment/Clubs	120	160	40
Cable & Internet	95	95	0
Other Expenses	0	150	150
Magazine Subscription	0	19	19
	547	567	20
Controllable Income:	509	417	92
Other Non-Reccurring Expenses			
Car Repair	230	0	230
Net Bank Account Increase/Decrease	279	417	138

Comparing your budget to actual performance will enable you to quickly be able to see where you spend too much and where you saved money. From the personal budget you will notice that compared to the corporate budget, revenue for "Johnny Charisma Doe" is fixed which means he is probably on a salary. Notice that rent is by far the biggest expense, taking up 26% of his total spending ability. One should note that Johnny actually did better than his budget but he incurred an unexpected car repair expense which made him underperform his budget. A proper budget should assume some buffer against one-off charges so that they can be absorbed in your savings plan throughout the year.

Ultimately, if one boldly assumes no other non-recurring expenses in the next 11 months, Johnny should achieve his target based on current spending. This conclusion can be drawn from:

Remaining Months in Year: 11 months
Controllable Income (from recent month): $509
Savings from current month: $279
Total savings for remainder of year: ($509*11) +$279 = $5,878

The resulting $5,878 means in the next 11 months he only has a buffer of $878 to cover any non-reoccurring expenditures. Therefore Johnny knows he spent over budget due to the car repair in August 2016 but he can be certain and confident he will be able to achieve his targeted savings if he remains disciplined in his spending practices.

Being confident in your budget enables you to be confident in what you can and can't afford. The trips you save up for could translate into you experiencing interesting things in life that not everyone can and most significantly share those memories with the important people you choose to let in your life. Self-confidence can stem from the bank account balance and this, in general, is a <u>bad thing</u>. If you suffer from low perceived self-worth, or rather low self-esteem, some extra money might make you feel better about yourself. But this is wrong. Generating any sense of self-value from an underlying bank account value is not healthy. Many men will feel unworthy of a woman just because his bank account is empty. The woman doesn't care that your bank account is empty but she will begin to care over time if you don't <u>take action</u> to change that. Creating a budget and ensuring you can be accountable to yourself for your spending practices shows that you're capable of self-restraint, discipline and even a little bit of financial savvy. How can you be a potential "head of household" if you can't even be accountable to yourself?

Alright, now, let's bring some of this money budget talk back to dating & social aspects. Yes, money can bring forth a sense of confidence because society values it so much. As mentioned at the onset of the Wealth section, money can't buy happiness...it also can't raise a family or make a woman fall in love with you. Ever try to approach a lady with "I'm so rich"? It won't work...well, it might work, but likely not for a long term relationship. If you haven't tried to open with that line you should, just to see the social pull away most women will react with. Bragging to a woman you don't know about material things at the start of a conversation is a sure way to either a.) Display how much you need the material thing to generate any sort of self-worth or confidence, or b.) Attract a gold digger. Whenever you brag, especially to someone you don't know, it's basically saying you need other people to validate how amazing you are because of something you have. Instead you should just be able to show them how amazing you are by taking action, and never feeling "threatened" enough to brag to anyone, ever, because you don't need that external validation. You know you are already a catch just by being the best version of yourself and constantly working to make yourself that much better regardless of who or what is around you. By being financially self-sufficient it makes you independent and that independence is attractive as you no longer need anything from anyone to survive on your own. It also shows you can rely on your own resourcefulness to get by in life and even prosper enough to invest in your own self-improvement.

W2 - Investments:

Now investments is after savings in this book for a reason. I believe, for most people, that one should only invest money that one saved; not borrowed. Moreover, one should not consider investing anything if they are barely able to achieve the first two tiers of Maslow's Hierarchy of Needs. Oddly enough as an accountant you would assume that with investments I would jump right into stocks/bonds & derivatives but the first thing you should do with any additional money you have as discretional is invest it in yourself.

So what does "investing in yourself" mean?

It means buying a self-help book and applying it to parts of your life. It means taking a one day workshop on how to be a leader. It means trying to take on a new skill set even though you think you might suck at it. It means taking a course part time. It means learning a new recipe. It means backpacking to remote places to learn about the world. It means learning how to change a tire. In short, investing can mean a lot of things, but investing in yourself is the best investment there is because you can take that investment with you everywhere you go.

These investments in yourself don't have to be big. While a four year degree can be a good investment it's also time consuming with a high opportunity cost. An opportunity cost is defined as the loss of potential gain from other alternatives when one alternative is chosen. Tuition is not an opportunity cost, it is rather a real outlay of cash. True cost of a four year degree is more accurately composed of both tuition and opportunity cost. In this example let an opportunity cost equate to the things you are forgoing because you are "forced" to study for this degree. In this case the opportunity cost would equal:

1.) Annual take home income of a fulltime job for <u>four</u> years.

2.) Less annual part time pay you would have earned as a student for <u>four</u> years.

3.) Plus an additional cost of other skill sets not learned due to the time commitment.

However, the larger the tuition plus opportunity cost the less likely <u>other</u> people would have incurred those costs to have those skills which could make the expected reward worth it if the skill you learned is scarce. In this example this means you will have to forecast the job market for your specific degree up to four years in advance. It should be noted many professional economists cannot generally accurately predict job markets one year in advance. Opportunity cost represents a natural trade-off so make sure you are aware the longer you are tied up with a personal investment in yourself the less able you are to learn others.

It is strongly encouraged that you create a small list of 3-5 skills you want to learn that are relatively easy to pick up yourself and add to that list each time you achieve one of those shortlisted skills. So if you finally learn to cook a turkey for your family that isn't burnt you can scratch that one off the list and jot down that you want to learn how to skate. Not only does this make it so you are constantly improving at a steady rate, but it is also motivating as each time you cross something off that list it serves as a visual representation of you actually becoming a better version of yourself. No matter how small the task, you will actually have a "guilty pleasure" crossing those learned skills off your list. Integrating this to the Social Pillar, is that this short list of skills can also be easily translated to fun first or second dates. For example, I remember putting "learn how to shoot a gun" and getting a lovely woman to join me as a date so we could learn together. Even though this lady kicked my ass at shooting a gun, it was still a date she is not likely to forget. Not only that but it also gave me the opportunity to tell the woman I have a dynamic short list of skills that I want to learn. This always resonated well with every woman I ever told that to. No woman ever said "that's a dumb idea"; in fact it usually made their eyes light up. Furthermore, this act also creates fun, interesting and different dates that other guys won't have the ingenuity to come up with. Most importantly you will automatically be driven to be present (S1.2) at the date since it's actually an activity you want to do or a skill you want to learn. Not only that but you can also link this investment in yourself to physical dates like rock climbing, archery and neon bowling. Now you are hitting all three pillars of self-improvement by just by reframing the idea of investment. Take a woman on a date to an activity you want to learn that gets your blood moving.

Now it's time to talk about investing in the standard banking and accounting sense. It is argued the allocation of money should be prioritized accordingly, top down, like this:

Covering basic needs.

Saving while investing in yourself.

Additional money committed to long term investment.

Therefore investments, like stocks and bonds, should only be considered when you have enough disposable income to cover your basic needs, savings goals and invest enough money back into yourself. I would note that investing in yourself does not have to cost money, it could also cost time (opportunity cost).

Assuming you have that additional monetary spillover, because of your income or spending discipline, you have managed to unlock the ability to invest for the future. From a self-help

212

perspective this should indicate that you currently have leftover money you were unable to invest immediately back into yourself so instead you invested it in your future. You could use this surplus money as a "canary" to determine if it's possible to better allocate that money to yourself now for better immediate skill building. The real question is why invest anything at all for your future if you're just going to die anyway? I mean no one says on their deathbed "I wish I made more money". Usually it's "I wish I spent more time with family", "I wish I would have traveled the world", "I wish I would have married for love". The primary reasons to invest in your future are two things a.) The money you currently have may not be there in the future (maybe your job or job market is unstable). b.) Retirement. Both reasons come from the acknowledgement that you may not make the same amount of money to sustain the current lifestyle you have. As a rule of thumb most people should strive to have a savings account with at least 8 months' worth of life support. That is in Johnny Charisma Doe's case (from August budget) he would need to cover Non-Discretional expenses and Discretional expenses for 8 months which is:

Non-Discretionary Expenses: $2,044
Discretionary Expenses: $547
Life Support Savings: ($2,044+$547)*8 month = $20,728

This assumes no non-reoccurring expenses, no unemployment social programs and no other interim sources of income while Mr. John Doe actively tries to get a similar position and income level at another company.

Investing for retirement is a challenge as you want to make sure you can sustain a standard of living when you are no longer working. Usually this comes in the form of a pension. In retired Johnny Charisma Doe's case we will assume his retirement pension is 60% of his current salary income $3,000*60% = $1,800 and that he no longer has rent expenses (Johnny was able to pay off his home by the time he retired). His budget would look something like what follows on the next page.

Income Statement
Retired Johnny "Charisma" Doe
Actual vs. Budgeted Variance Analysis
For the month of August 31, 2016

	Actual	Budgeted	Variance
Revenue	1,800	1,800	0
Non-Discretionary Spending			
Meals	160	170	10
Utilities (Water, Sewage, Power)	370	400	30
Cell Phone	80	80	0
Vehicle Payment	106	106	0
Vehicle Insurance	120	120	0
Property Tax	200	200	0
Total Essential Spending:	1,036	1,076	40
Total Income After Essentials	764	724	40
Discretionary Spending			
Going out meals	200	73	127
Gym membership	50	50	0
Gas for Car	150	60	90
Medical Expenses	90	216	126
Gifts for Friends/Shopping	150	120	30
Entertainment	50	60	10
Donations	95	95	0
Other Expenses	0	50	50
Total Discretional Expenses:	787	724	63
Controllable Income:	-23	0	-23
Other Non-Recurring Expenses	0	0	0
Net Bank Account Increase/Decrease	-23	0	-23

In Johnny's case you should notice that he is no longer trying to save any money and wants to spend close to what his pension income is. You should also notice that if he was still paying rent, Johnny would not be able to sustain his lifestyle for very long. Johnny has also started to invest in others by increasing donations and gifts to his loved ones and family members.

When you retire hopefully you find yourself in Johnny's situation where he can start investing in others because he was smart enough to invest in himself early on. So how can you ensure you are able to retire like Johnny and help other's invest in themselves to better them just like you bettered yourself? Assuming you make/save enough for self-actualization to occur it's finally time to invest in the stock market.

Technology has made investing in most major stock markets very easy. So should you do it yourself?

The average person nowadays can make investment decisions for themselves. It has yet to be statistically proven that the average investment banker can beat that of a monkey at picking stocks over a longer length of time. Princeton professor Burton Malkiel goes so far as to argue in his 1973 bestseller "A Random Walk Down Wall Street" that a "Blindfolded monkey throwing darts at a newspaper's financial pages could select a portfolio that would do just as well as one carefully selected by experts."

So why pay someone 2% of your return on investment each year for adding zero value?

The main argument for going to an investment professional firm in this day and age is that they:

1.) Already have a diversified pool of assets and portfolios.

2.) Provide liquidity that you could not replicate alone.

3.) Tailor investments that are right for your personality type and investment needs.

These services are important. Determining if an investment firm is the right decision for your money is contingent on if you think you can do the above three things yourself. Investment firms also help free up time. You won't have to be always thinking about how your investments are doing.

Alternatively, if you are anything like me, and always want to know what your investments are doing and be in direct control of buying and selling investments within seconds, then it may be better to set up your own trading account. This also makes you more accountable for what you decide to invest in and forces you not to "play the victim" and blame some third party who likely won't care half as much about how your investments perform as you would.

In finance <u>the reason why investments yield any type of return is because of underlying risk</u>. No one gets anything for nothing. This is a critical principle. Make sure you understand that before you invest anything. As stated, you should only be in a position to invest after basic needs have been met and you have already started to invest in yourself. Investing has no guarantees and therefore you have to ask yourself "if my investment goes to zero how would I react? Would my life change?" If an investment is too critical for your overall wellbeing than you probably have too much invested in that company. Take investment with an "only invest what I can afford to lose" philosophy. This makes investments naturally much less emotional and more cognitively driven. Instead of being forced to sell when an investment goes wrong you can instead more calmly determine why the investment is going off the mark and conclude if the idea is wrong or just your timing. If the idea is still sound, technically assuming all else equal, the investment simply just got cheaper and it's a potential opportunity to add more money into your idea at a cheaper price.

In the world of finance there are a few and far between hard truths and theories that stand the test of time that everyone can agree upon. <u>Diversification is one of these hard proofs</u>. It has been proven that diversifying allows you to reduce your portfolio risk while not sacrificing your return. That is to say company specific risk can be diversified away the more stocks you own, assuming you are not investing in all similar companies in similar industries with similar business risks. This power of diversification becomes marginally less each time you effectively diversify with some papers sourcing 30 stocks are enough to effectively diversify company specific risk assuming low correlation between the stocks. Technology has utilized this theory of diversification so today one can simply buy 30 stocks on their own and effectively diversify themselves without paying 2% of your return to an investment firm. While that 2% seems small, for perspective, assuming the average yearly return is somewhere between 6-8% a year. That's 25 - 33% of your return going to someone that's not you... even though you are the one bearing all the investment risk. The bank won't reimburse you if you lose your investment, so why should they get rewarded 25% of the return? The Average Joe will not be able to effectively diversify into 30 stocks off the start, especially because most banks charge between $5–$10 per trade on average. Technology again, however, has made it so you can effectively diversify into a stock that passively reflects markets. You can actually invest in the entire market or specific industries of a market for a third of the price most active investment brokers will charge you. These investment vehicles are called ETF's (Exchange-Traded Fund) and the most common one is arguably denominated with the stock symbol SPY. This ETF replicates that of the entire Standard & Poor's 500 index. I will speak more about the perks of an ETF strategy later.

Recall, the third most important function a good investment company will do is tailor your personality to your investment needs. This can also be accomplished yourself by reflecting and judging how risk averse you are. Ultimately, how well you do this is up to your honest, unbiased judgement of yourself or up to a good investment company's software. If you do decide to go the route of an investment company, remember nothing is risk free that generates a return. Even AAA credit ranked government bonds in developed countries have a degree of risk associated with them. Countries do default, read Roger Lowenstein's, "When Genius Failed: The Rise and Fall of Long-Term Capital Management" if you don't believe me...so don't let anyone tell you otherwise.

Since everyone is different, and different people have different risk tolerances and different required rates of return it is extremely difficult to tell you what to invest in. That being said, I will provide the jest of what you should know to "Do It Yourself" (DIY), or at least make sure an investment company will not be able to take advantage of a lack of investment knowledge. Three basic types of investments are "Risk Free Assets", Bonds, and Stocks. This book will assume the average reader who would pick up a self-help book and its interrelation with dating is probably aged 21-38. That being said "Risk Free Assets" and Bonds are consequently and arguably not for you.

"Risk free" investments are investments like Federal Government bonds. That is investing in the debt of the government. I would like you to note that the term "risk free" is a lie. Nothing gives a return that is risk free as this violates the principal rule in finance; however, government bonds typically give a low guaranteed rate of return which many finance models use as the "risk free rate". This is why investment gurus use the term "risk free rate" even though a true risk free rate cannot exist. For my average reader I would argue not to invest in risk free assets for two main reasons:

1.) Government Bonds still have the default risk of the underlying government who issues the debt.

2.) Risk free investments generally are not indexed to inflation. Meaning if inflation increases, you could generate a return less than the cost of living increased. While you gained money, you gained less than what prices of goods on average increased by. So you actually lost money on a real dollar basis.

Bonds are similar to risk free assets but typically are composed of the debt of corporations. Corporate debt introduces a higher degree of default and credit risk. Like government bonds, you are investing in debt but this time of an individual company, which, unlike the government can't print money or lower interest rates on a macroeconomic scale and thus lower their interest rate payments. This increase in risk generates a higher fixed rate of return. The more high risk the company is the more return you are likely to be compensated with for buying the company's debt. Bonds are generally best suited for investors who are older, have a shorter time horizon and are planning to retire in the near future. These investors are people that want smaller fixed amount of income each year from investments. Like risk free assets, most general corporate bonds are susceptible to inflation risk and interest rate risk. Which means the $5 you earned on a $100 bond last year may not cover the fact that what $100 in general goods you bought last year now will cost you $110. So in real terms you lost $5 in purchasing power despite your investment performing as expected.

Stocks are the best vehicle to invest in for the average reader and targeted audience of this book. As mentioned earlier, a portfolio with 30 different stocks with little correlation between them yields a risk/return ratio that surpasses most. There are many different ways to invest in stocks. ETF's as mentioned earlier are a quick, relatively cheap way to diversify in the stock market without having to do research on individual companies. Some of the most common and liquid ETF symbols are SPY, IWN, QQQ & DIA. These all replicate certain markets without having to own each company in said market. This is by far the easiest way to diversify away company specific risk and utilize the proven power of diversification while paying a much smaller fee to the ETF owner than what an investment company would charge to actively manage and allocate your money. There are also industry specific ETF's which allow you to "diversify" to the extent of that specific industry. Stocks are the proposed investment type for anyone not planning to retire in 5 -10 years for a variety of reasons. Stocks partially hedge against inflation given that a stock price rises as inflation increases due to companies increasing their earnings due to inflation. That being said, often times a small portion of assets should be allocated to bonds if only for diversification purposes as bonds and stocks generally have a lower correlation with each other than that of other stocks. I would note here that if you do go the route of ETF's be careful around leveraged ETF's. Not only is there a time decay (not useful for holding in the long-term) but they also use derivatives to provide their leverage, which means little to no dividend income. This brings me to one of the best parts of investing in stocks...the dividends.

Dividends, for the context of this book, are simply extra money a successful company is able to reward its shareholders for holding its common stock. Usually larger, more mature, established companies, regulated utilities or real estate investment trusts (REIT), pay steady dividends which can be pivotal in your investment decisions. Many companies are actually valued on their current dividend and what the projected dividend is likely to be in the future, which illustrates just how important this dividend can be for underlying market value/share price.

Below is an over-simplified illustration, not drawn to scale, which just serves to reinforce the superiority of stocks over a long period of time and why I suggest them to my average reader:

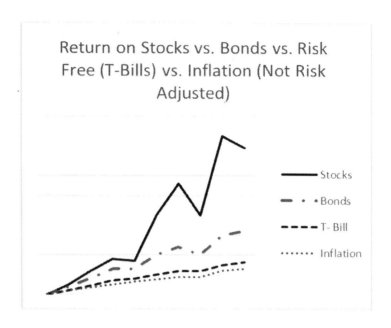

Return on Stocks vs. Bonds vs. Risk Free (T-Bills) vs. Inflation (Not Risk Adjusted)

As illustrated, one would expect stocks to outperform on a return-level basis if only to be compensated for the higher risk stocks have associated with them. Remember, if a company goes bankrupt typically the stock is worth zero but the debt holders may be able to get something back from the company. Stocks are riskier than both government and corporate debt. This relationship is exemplified above and aligns with the primary finance principal that risk generates return.

However, in the long run, historically speaking, stocks have outperformed all other basic vehicles of investment on even a risk adjusted basis. This means over a longer holding period, the risk/return trade off of stocks is superior to bonds and "risk free assets". Which translates to the fact that historically, stocks provide more return per unit of risk than the other two vehicles of investment's discussed. As Jeremy Siegel, professor of Finance at the Wharton School of University of Pennsylvania wrote in "Stocks for the Long Run", at a very long horizon stocks outperform bonds with almost 100% probability. So with some degree of certainty (which is rare in finance) it is suggested, assuming you are planning to hold onto a stock for ten years or more, that stocks are the superior way to invest and should be heavily weighted (90-100%) in any younger individual's portfolio.

International stocks also increase the diversification potential of most portfolios. It is actually possible to reduce the portfolio risk level below the domestic-only portfolio risk level by introducing foreign stocks into your investment. Be aware that if you do invest internationally you add additional political risk and foreign exchange risk to your portfolio. Taking on these additional risks may not be worth it. Furthermore, qualitatively, it is likely you may know less about the actual business if it is a foreign entity. The typical trade off with foreign investments is increased diversification vs. political and currency risk. Some international markets may not have an accounting framework in place. Be careful. This means the numbers that you and others rely on to make investments may not be accurate to a higher standard. Remember how women hate fake men? Well investors hate fake numbers. When investors find out the numbers are manipulated, the stock price almost always falls sharply. Most of the developed nations have rules about how a company has to present their financial statements. These companies spend billions of dollars in auditing and accounting costs annually just to meet these rules so they can maintain their stock on the exchange for an alternative avenue of funding. They would not spend this money if they didn't think they had to.

People can pick and value stocks based on a variety of measures (like dividends) and investment viewpoints. If you do decide not to use an investment firm or buy a passive ETF the only thing I want to make clear is that you diversify. Pick stocks that don't all move in step with each other and make sure you do your research on each individual company you decide to take ownership in. Understand why people or other companies are buying from this prospective company.

If you do take a do-it-yourself approach to investing, which I think every individual should to some degree, try to make a portfolio of stocks that's right for you. Consider that you can always invest some of your earnings passively through an ETF and manage the rest actively yourself so that you still get some tangible investment experience and hold yourself accountable for your investment decisions. Doing that will ensure some degree of diversification while also increasing your skills and knowledge investment base. Thus, making yourself a better investor in real time while making sure you don't risk it all while you are still learning. In short I am suggesting to do a <u>mixed strategy</u> if you do decide to do it yourself. <u>Index the core of your portfolio (in a cheap diversified ETF) and then try the stock picking game for money you can afford to put at higher risk.</u> Therefore you dilute your risk while improving your investing knowledge by getting your hands dirty directly. This direct action makes you accountable, able to influence your own investments and weightings in each stock and physically makes you in charge of your future in the finance realm of your life. This increase in knowledge through taking action, while holding yourself accountable, will lead to an overall increase in skill when it comes to handling money naturally. This will make you more robust financially, and like any increase in skill, will generally lead to an overall increase in confidence in your ability to manage money overtime.

W2.1 Additional Investment Advice For The DIY In You

- Invest in things you know. Don't just understand what the company sells. Understand who is buying the products, where the products are coming from and what makes them better than the competition.

- Ask yourself how easy is it for another company to come in and fulfill the role the company you are thinking about investing in is currently providing. Identify if the services/goods your firm provides is easily replicated. If there are high barriers of entry then visualize that your investment is a castle and that high barrier of entry is a moat around it that is not easy to lay siege to. A higher barrier of entry produces less company specific risk and should translate to an increase in pricing power and therein profitability.

- Investments are investing in the future. Make sure you understand that when you invest you are buying what people think the company is likely to be worth in the future, not what it is worth today.

- Don't invest too much in the company you work for. If you get let go because the company is struggling, you can get hit twice as hard when that company's share price starts failing.

- Don't assume you know more than everyone else. Ego, just like in dating, is the enemy; avoid it.

- Know what industry you are investing in. Some industries, like tech and pharmaceutical companies, provide higher risk (and therefore reward) as earnings and moreover, perceived future earnings, have a colossal effect on share price performance. In contrast, utility stocks typically are less sensitive and less risky as the market has an easier time pricing these companies due to the fact that they are relatively unlikely to change dramatically each year going forward.

- Understand technological threats to your investment. Will a certain technological advancement slowly take away business or replace an existing good/service?

- Don't do something just because somebody else is doing it.

- Always do your own personal due diligence on each company as you are putting your own hard earned money on the line.

- Trade as little as possible. Nowadays transaction fees can take large cuts out of your return. Buy and Hold strategies often outperform many other more active strategies and this is largely attributed to the high cost of transaction fees.

- Review your investments at least once a year so you can keep up on any changes in the corporation. I personally check my investments each day, but do quarterly reviews on price targets and review if the underlying explanation for my initial investment has been altered.

- "...You want to be greedy when others are fearful" – Warren Buffet (American business magnate, investor and philanthropist). Unjustified group fear in the market can be an opportunity.

- When an investment goes poorly ask yourself why it did so and if this poor performance in share price is legitimate or presents further opportunity.

- Don't try to time the market. This is when you stop investing and start speculating.

- Don't just buy a company because it dropped by a large percent recently. Usually these drops reflect underlying issues with the company that the market didn't previously realize. However, this can still be an opportunity if there is market overreaction to the bad news.

- Know your exit strategy when you buy an investment. Have an idea where you see the stock going and how much you will take out of your investment when it gets there. Stick to that initial price target. If you become greedy, a gain on paper might as well be imaginary. It is not the same as a gain converted back into cash (realized gain).

As a side note, most modern countries tax investments at a lesser rate than other sources of income. That is, gains from investments and dividend income are taxed at a rate that is less than your typical income tax rate, say from a job. This favorable tax rate should not influence your decision to invest but it should motivate you to put yourself in a position where you can invest more in your future. Having more income derived from investment will, as a percentage, decrease your marginal tax rate. In short, in most of the developed nations, the more of your income that comes from investments leads to an overall decrease in your personal marginal tax rate.

There are some final closing remarks I can't understate enough. Shares are priced based on <u>future expectations</u>. In Benjamin Graham's book, "The Interpretation of Financial Statements," he expressly states:

"Broadly speaking, the price of common stocks is governed by the prospective earnings. These prospective earnings are a matter of estimation or foresight and the action of the stock market on this point is usually controlled by the indicated trend."

Keep in mind that trends can change and this means all current share prices are based on estimates of the future. The greater the uncertainty of the future for any given company, the more risky and thus potentially rewarding the stock will be. The price of common stocks will depend not so much on previous or present earnings but what people think the future earnings will be. This means people come from a future mindset when it comes to investment. Therefore investments will naturally take you away from being present. So don't be checking your stocks when you decide to set a date with your dream girl.

Given the current price of a stock is dictated by the current trend you need to always ask yourself two key questions before you hit that "buy" button:

1.) How confident are you that this trend will remain into the future?

2.) How hefty a price are you paying in advance for the estimated continuance of the trend?

Again to quote Benjamin Graham who I should mention is also coined the "Father of Value Investing" and more well known for his influence on Warren Buffet:

"At bottom the ability to buy securities-particularly common stocks – successfully is the ability to look ahead accurately. Looking backward, however carefully, will not suffice, and may do more harm than good. Common stock selection is a difficult art – naturally, since it offers large rewards for success. It requires a skillful mental balance between the facts of the past and the possibilities of the future."

If planning to go down the DIY route of investing, I highly suggest reading Benjamin Graham's book, "The Intelligent Investor" to assist in avoiding common dangers.

W2.2 Avoid Psychological Investment Pitfalls

The following are all investment pitfalls I have personally struggled with and quite honestly still fall victim to occasionally despite knowing about them. Interesting, like the common relationship mistakes at the end of the Social Pillar the investment pitfalls are also largely linked to having an ego.

- Disposition Effect: Investors tend to sell winners too early and hold losers too long. Selling winners validates your decision to purchase the stock in the first place while selling losers admits that your decision to buy it was a bad choice. The disposition effect is ego. Selling winners early validates the ego and never selling losers preserves the ego. This idea can be linked to the Prospect Theory originally put forth by Kahneman and Tversky in "Prospect Theory: An Analysis of Decision under Risk" published back in 1979. Daniel Kahneman actually ended up winning the 2002 Nobel Memorial Prize in Economics based on the idea of Prospect Theory, so if you find behavioural finance interesting I highly suggest reading this article.

- Cognitive Dissonance: Remembering only what you want to remember. While it is difficult to admit when you made an error, don't dissociate with your error. Embrace it and learn from the error so that you don't make it again. Lying to yourself only does yourself injustice.

- House Money Effect: Investors become more risk taking after recent gains. This idea originates from Richard Thaler and Eric Johnson's scholarly article "Gambling with the House Money and Trying to Break even". People under sway of the "house money effect" can fall victim to having a higher risk tolerance for money your investments already made. This is irrational. The money you made from your investments is your money as you took the risk to make it. Don't treat it separately as the "house's" money.

- Overconfidence: Investors tend to be overconfident about their investment skill. Don't let your ego defeat your investments. Like the social aspect of this book, destroy the ego of overconfidence by treating success with modesty and not identifying with your success at a personal level. The best way to defeat overconfidence is simply to write off any success as luck. Attributing your success to other people will also effectively reduce your ego while making others feel appreciated. The trick here is that you actually have to genuinely believe your success was attributable to external sources.

While investments in stocks can be rewarding, as Benjamin Franklin once said, an "investment in knowledge pays the most interest". That is, investment in stocks should be secondary to investment in yourself. Skill building and being the best version of yourself is critical in order to live a healthy, more robust and well-rounded life. A woman won't care that your $10,000 in Apple increased 5% today, but she will care if you put that $500 towards a spontaneous trip to the mountains with just the two of you or to a three-day seminar on "insert skill-you –want-to-learn-together here".

Money, just like alcohol, can be a crutch for meeting women if you let it, and can even be more toxic than booze ever could be to your potential relationships. Men can develop an ego and a self-worth that is derived from numbers on a bank account balance. Women will be able to tell you need them to see that you have money in order for you to generate any type of self-worth. Moreover, it could indicate you value money so much so that it is likely you would compromise your integrity to make a quick buck. By extension it would also mean you would be insecure if someone with more money started just talking to your girlfriend. This introduces a type of comparison paradigm where no one wins as someone will always have more money. As Nobel Prize winner Earnest Hemingway proclaimed: "There is nothing noble in being superior to your fellow man; true nobility is being superior to your former self." Beat comparison paradigms by accepting the fact that you can only control yourself. If you want to compare yourself to anything, compare yourself to yesterday's version of you. Once you have enough money it should be viewed as "c'est la vie" and ultimately unimportant in your overall dating life; not a source of validation. Meaning after you meet or date and determine any type of connection or chemistry then, and only then, do you show that you can also fulfill the provider role. Not the other way around. Some people show the provider role first and that tends to lead to an overall decrease in sexual chemistry for the rest of the relationship's time fused life.

In closing off the Wealth Pillar, money should be viewed as a tool to unlock access to better Health and Social wellbeing. Money allows you to invest in yourself, your family and gives you the opportunity to focus and build on yourself for the future instead of just living day by day. As illustrated by Maslow's Hierarchy we need a certain amount of financial security and stability to truly take root and begin the journey towards self-actualization via the process of constant self-improvement. Money in of itself should not be used to brag or as a crutch for personal validation. Money is not happiness but it makes it much easier to obtain it. It is ironic that money can make things easier to obtain...but the fact that things become easier to obtain makes it less likely that you will value the things you buy. Worse still, money can isolate you by creating trust issues with friends and family members and can even be the foundation of paranoia and even depression. Is that one specific woman you actually really like into you or just into the fact that you slaved away for a decade and saved $300,000 while she partied the last decade away and is finally ready to settle down and have children? These ugly thoughts show that money can be a double edged sword. It is argued that having enough money to survive and a bit more to invest in what you want to do with your own life whilst taking care of your family is probably the ideal amount you would want. Anything more has marginally decreasing returns on happiness while the opportunity cost of making said extra money becomes too high. You only have so many years to live so strike a balance and strive to be the best version of you...not the richest. And as one of the most famous economists ever, John Maynard Keynes, once said, "In the long run we are all dead."

CONCLUSION

By mastering these three Pillars of Social, Health and Wealth, maximizing your ability to be a better you and measuring your progress in meaningful ways I hope you are able to unlock a more successful you...Well maybe not successful, given the subjectivity of the word, but at least on track to being a better version of yourself. I really do believe the focus on Social, Health and Wealth will make you stronger, confident, well-rounded and overall more attractive to the opposite sex. As for me, I will view success as anyone who utilizes any of these tools in this book and comes out the better for it.

Just remember women don't want the perfect man...they want the man who is perfectly fine with himself.

On the next page is a "By Being Code" of sorts. This code does not have to be specific to dating, I found it helped me ensure I was being the "sun" and not the "black hole". In general, society often favors, and materially rewards, people for putting one over on others, which actively promotes the creation of more structurally sound black hole individuals. I have chosen the road of giving back to others for the selfish purpose of keeping that positive feedback loop spiral going upward. This "code" on the following page helped me stay more "sun" like and helped me out when I wasn't sure what to do in my dating life.

The Sun Framework

By being:

Abundant, you are not needy, creepy, clingy or reaction seeking.

Present, you are sharp, ready, spontaneous, fun and carefree.

Sincerely Congruent, you are authentic, grounded and confident in yourself.

Engaging, you are unstifled, fun and genuinely interested in your potential life partner.

The source of emotion, you dictate the emotions of the interaction.

Active, you force genuine, in the moment, interactions.

Assertive, you form an identity for someone to truly start knowing who you are.

Outcome independent, you become fearless and self-reliant.

Transparently Clear In Your Intent, you become goal oriented, focused, and much more able.

A Leader, you are comfortable with being responsible for more than just your own actions.

By being these things you will carry value into any interactions you find yourself in.

Amplifying these Core Social Skills while visually displaying self-improvement through disciplined and regimental diet and exercise is a great way to put your money where your mouth is. A healthier you makes you happier, a happier you makes you have any easier time demonstrating higher value in all your interactions. Leverage the fact that you take care of yourself and bring it to your social interactions. Good health has numerous beneficial intricacies, as mentioned, that weave their way back into your social life.

Finally, distinguishing value from money for social interactions, means you remove the socially accepted standard for success and wellbeing and replace it with your own measurements of self-worth. Value is not derived from what someone else says you are worth. Excessive amounts of money will not make you excessively happy. However, a lack of resources will lead to the inability to focus on self-improvement, dating and limit the experiences you can provide for others and yourself.

Some parts of "The Reframe" can be directly associated with picking up women; that being said, as stated throughout, the intention of this book is simply to be the best version of yourself and that should set the stage for a stronger, more robust, more meaningful relationships with others. As mentioned, I acknowledge and accept that parts of this book may go against social norms. However, I believe that when social relationships aren't exactly working as intended (i.e. high divorce rate) some rethinking/reframing is more than warranted. I wrote this book to help as many people as I could ensure they are equipped to find a life partner that they truly desire. Together, in reframing how we view relationships from a man's perspective, I hope we can bring that staggering divorce statistic back down. There is something broken here and we need to fix it; something crooked that needs to be leveled out.

Personally, I would take great pleasure in getting feedback from you after reading my book, "The Reframe" and applying these concepts in your journey towards finding a potential life partner. Below is a link to my Facebook, Twitter & Amazon pages:

Facebook: https://www.facebook.com/TheReframe

Twitter: https://twitter.com/B_Matha_Maddox

Twitter Handle: @B_Matha_Maddox.

Amazon: https://www.amazon.com/author/brianmaddox

Feel free to message me questions about the book on any of these platforms.

Going forward, don't be complacent. Be determined. At all times, not stopping when you've seized your goal. "Though one may seem to have attained success for the moment, one will start to regress the instant one becomes careless and ceases making effort, beginning a slide toward defeat," writes Buddhist spiritual leader Daisaku Ikeda. Complacency is the seed of stagnancy and within it will grow ego that will attempt to play it safe and maintain the progress you have worked so hard to achieve. Keep progressing. Not maintaining. Always. Only then will you never truly stop growing as a person.

Never stop improving.

Reframe yourself.

Reframe relationships.

Reframe society.

APPENDIX

The following pages are Appendices for quick references to key visual concepts in the book. These are enclosed for readers who may want to access certain charts or ideas more efficiently when out and about in the world searching for your potential significant other.

Appendix 1:

The Sun Framework

By being:

1.) Abundant, you are not needy, creepy, clingy or reaction seeking.

2.) Present, you are sharp, ready, spontaneous, fun and carefree.

3.) Sincerely Congruent, you are authentic, grounded and confident in yourself.

4.) Engaging, you are unstifled, fun and genuinely interested in your potential life partner.

5.) The source of emotion, you dictate the emotions of the interaction.

6.) Active, you force genuine, in the moment, interactions.

7.) Assertive, you form an identity for someone to truly start knowing who you are.

8.) Outcome independent, you become fearless and self-reliant.

9.) Transparently Clear In Your Intent you become goal oriented, focused, and much more able.

10.) A Leader, you are comfortable with being responsible for more than just your own actions.

By being these things you will carry value into any interactions you find yourself in.

Appendix 2:

Caloric Deficit Chart

WEIGHT/ HEIGHT*	5'8	5'10	5'11	6
210	1,904	1,936	1,952	1,968
205	1,881	1,913	1,929	1,945
200	1,859	1,890	1,906	1,922
195	1,836	1,868	1,883	1,900
190	1,813	1,845	1,861	1,877
185	1,790	1,822	1,838	1,854
180	1,768	1,799	1,815	1,831
175	1,745	1,778	1,794	1,808
170	1,721	1,754	1,770	1,788
165	1,700	1,730	1,747	1,763
160	1,677	1,709	1,724	1,740
155	1,654	1,686	1,702	1,716
150	1,630	1,663	1,679	1,695
145	1,609	1,640	1,656	1,672
140	1,586	1,618	1,632	1,650

*This schedule assumes age 28, male with no physical activity outside of resting.

As mentioned in this book, this chart is an approximation. Everyone is physically different. This chart roughly estimates how many calories you can eat and ensure you are still in a deficit. This information comes from Freedieting.com. These numbers assume no physical activity, so if you have a physical job you would need to eat much more or risk losing a large amount of muscle and fat. It is recommended to enter your own body information into this calculator to help get an idea of what is a realistic caloric intake for your goals.

Appendix 3:

Determining Body Fat Percentage

Body Fat %	General Waist Measurement*
5-6% bf	Waist is 41.8% of height. If 5'10 = 170Cm * 41.8% = 71.06 cm =28.0 Inch Waist
6-7% bf	Waist is 42.1% of height. If 5'10 = 170Cm * 42.1% = 71.57 cm =28.2 Inch Waist
7-8% bf	Waist is 42.5% of height. If 5'10 = 170Cm * 42.5% = 72.25 cm =28.5 Inch Waist
8-9% bf	Waist is 43.0% of height. If 5'10 = 170Cm * 43.0% = 73.10 cm =28.9 Inch Waist
9-10% bf	Waist is 43.6% of height. If 5'10 = 170Cm * 43.6% = 74.12 cm =29.2 Inch Waist
10-12% bf	Waist is 44.7% of height. If 5'10 = 170Cm * 44.7% = 75.99 cm =29.9 Inch Waist
12-14% bf	Waist is 45.7% of height. If 5'10 = 170Cm * 45.7% = 77.69 cm =30.6 Inch Waist

*These measurements would be skewed if one has a highly developed core. For the average reader, using waist as a percentage of height is a good way to estimate your body fat percentage without the use of tools. This table is slightly tweaked, but originates from Radu Antoniu's concept of targeting a specific waist size and estimating body fat percentage by using your waist as a percent of your height. Radu Antoniu is a recommended YouTube persona and author at "Think Eat Lift".

Recognize that this table is a crude approximation.

Appendix 4:

Strength Goals – Absolute & Relative

Absolute Strength Targets:

Typically there are absolute targets in the gym one could strive for. Such as:

- 315 Pound Deadlift

- 280 Pound Squat

- 200 Pound Bench Press

Relative Strength Targets:

Exercise (5 reps)	Very Fit	Intermediate	Advanced
Incline Bench Press	95% of Body Weight	120% body Weight	140% Body Weight
Weighted Chin Ups	30% Body Weight Added	40% Body Weight Added	65% Body Weight Added
Standing Shoulder Press	65% Body Weight	80% Body Weight	100% Body Weight
Bicep Curls	60% Body Weight	70% Body Weight	75% Body Weight

These relative strength goals are primarily based off of Kinobody's Greg O'Gallaghers strength goals and are adjusted slightly based on personal experience and other various readings. Remember, relative strength is an approximate measure of what your physique likely looks like. Use these rough estimates as goals and guidelines to target specific body types you desire.

Appendix 5:

Expected Rate of Muscle Growth per Month

Category	Max Rate of Muscle Growth per Month
Beginner (Low amount of existing muscle):	1.1-1.5% Growth of Lean Body Mass
Intermediate (5'10, 170 pounds 12% BF)*	0.4%-1% Growth of Lean Body Mass
Advanced (5'10, 180 pounds 10% BF)*	0.2%-0.35% Growth of Lean Body Mass

*These categories are subjective and the examples in the intermediate and advanced categories should be taken with a grain of salt. These rates of growth are rough estimates based on Alan Aragorn's information in his book "Girth Control", and tailored slightly based on personal experience.

Use this chart to as a loose indicator to determine if the weight you are putting on is really muscle or just fat. Estimate your lean body mass by first determining your likely body fat percentage. Then subtract your total weight by the amount that is likely fat. This is your lean body mass.

Appendix 6:

Weekly Workout Routine:

Remember to use a workout routine that works for you. Use the below template if you are struggling or just starting off. If your schedule only allows you to go to the gym 3-4 times a week ensure you hit the big compound tracked movements before the smaller muscle groups.

Proposed Potential Workout Routine

Sunday	Monday	Tuesday	Wednesday	Thursday	Friday
Barbell Squat (*)	Standing Shoulder Press (*)	Weighted Chin Up (*)	Barbell Bench Press(*)	Weighted Triceps Dip	Deadlift (*)
Leg Press	Military Press (*)	Ez Curl Bar Bicep Curl(*)	Timed 100 Push Ups	Cable Push-Down	Wide-Grip Pull Up
Seated Leg Curl	Bent-Over Rear Delt Raise	Overhead Cable Curl	Peck Deck Machine	Skull-crushers	Bent-Over Barbell Row
Seated Leg Extension	Lateral Raise	Preacher Curl	Seated Machine Chest Press	Seated Overhead Dumbbell Extension	Wide-Grip Seated Cable Row
Standing Calf Raise	Reverse Machine Fly	Incline Hammer Curls	Low Cable Cross Over	Close-Grip Bench Press	Standing T-Bar Row

(*) = Track progress.

Appendix 7:

Maslow's Hierarchy of Needs

It's hard to plan for the future if you are struggling on a day to day basis. Money is more meaningful when you have less of it. Being forced to provide basic needs automatically makes one present. This is due to your body's hardwiring not allowing one to think about the future if it is worried about the present.

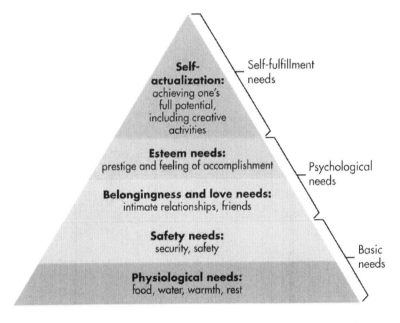

As already mentioned, the above picture is from simplypsychology.org. The pyramid correlates well with the theory that happiness as a function of money increases at a decreasing rate.

Appendix 8:

Division of Intent

Be clear in what you want. Don't have one foot on the gas and the other on the break. Know what your intention is going into an interaction. This clarity will make you focus and your efforts will cease to be divided. If you find yourself mentally exhausted after cold approaching a few women you are interested in, then chances are you were either not true to your intent, or rather not congruent with your intentions.

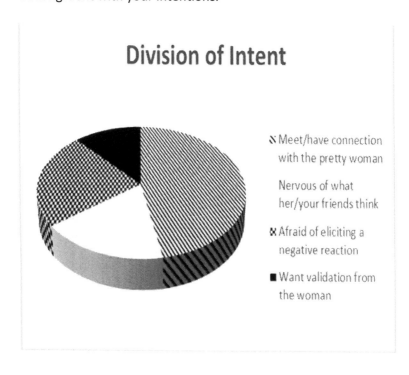

Appendix 9

Example of an Intermittent Fasting Schedule

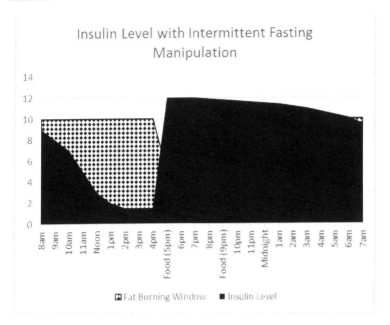

Insulin Level with Intermittent Fasting Manipulation

Be careful. Make sure your body can handle this type of stressor. Not having constant food and instant gratification can be a shock to your body if you currently over indulge in life's comforts. A fast, as indicated in the body of the book, does not need to be as rigid as what is illustrated above.

Appendix 10 – DIY Investment Tips

- Invest in things you know. Don't just understand what the company sells. Understand who is buying the products, where the products are coming from and what makes them better than the competition.

- Ask yourself how easy is it for another company to come in and fulfill the role the company you invested in is currently providing. Identify if the services/goods your firm provides is easily replicated. If there are high barriers of entry then visualize that your investment is a castle and that high barrier of entry is a moat around it that is not easy to lay siege to. A high barrier of entry creates less company specific risk and should translate to an increase in pricing power and therein profitability.

- Investments are investing in the future. Make sure you understand that when you invest you are buying what people think the company is likely to be worth in the future, not what it is worth today.

- Don't invest too much in the company you work for. If you get let go because the company is struggling you can get hit twice as hard when that company's share price starts failing.

- Don't assume you know more than everyone else. Ego, just like in dating, is the enemy; avoid it.

- Know what industry you are investing in. Some industries, like tech and pharmaceutical companies provide higher risk (and therefore reward) as earnings and moreover, perceived future earnings have a colossal effect on share price performance. In contrast, utility stocks and consumer staples typically are less sensitive and less risky as the market has an easier time pricing these companies due to the fact that they are relatively unlikely to change dramatically each year going forward.

- Understand technological threats to your investment. Will a certain technological advancement slowly take away business or replace an existing good/service.

- Don't do something just because somebody else is doing it.

- Always do your due diligence on each company as you are putting your hard earned money on the line.

- Trade as little as possible. Transaction fees can take large cuts out of your return. Buy and Hold strategies often outperform many other more active strategies and this is largely attributed to the high cost of transaction fees.

- Review your investments at least once a year so you can keep up on any changes in the corporation. I personally check my investments each day but do quarterly reviews.

- Be greedy when others are fearful. Fear can be an opportunity.

- When an investment goes poorly ask yourself why it did so and if this poor performance presents in share price is legitimate or presents further opportunity.

- Don't try to time the market. This is when you stop investing and start speculating.

- Don't buy a company just because it dropped by a large percent recently. Usually these drops reflect underlying issues with the company that the market didn't previously realize.

- Know your exit strategy when you buy an investment.

Appendix 11 – Recommended Books & Bibliography

As mentioned in the introduction many of these books below played a pivotal role in reinforcing various Social, Health and Wealth concepts throughout "The Reframe".

Aragon, Alan. 2007. *Girth Control: The Science of Fat Loss & Muscle Gain*. Alan Aragon.

Atkinson M, Mitchell J, Muir D, Passer M, Smith R. 2011. *Psychology: Frontiers and Applications*. Text Book. McGraw-Hill Ryerson Higher Education. Fourth Edition

Burton, Malkiel. 2012. *A Random Walk Down Wall Street: The Time-Tested Strategy for Successful Investing*. W.W. Norton & Co, Inc.

Carnegie, Dale. 1998. *How to Win Friends and Influence People*. Gallery Books. Special Anniversary Edition.

Covey, Stephen. 2004. *The 7 Habits of Highly Effective People*. Simon & Schuster, Inc.

Craighero L, Rizzolatti G. 2004. *The Mirror-Neuron System. Annual Review of Neuroscience.* Scholarly Article. Italy: University of Parma.

Deida, David. 2004. *The Way of the Superior Man*. Sounds True, Inc.

Graham B, Meredith S, Price M. 1998. *The Interpretation of Financial Statements*. HarperCollins Publishers Inc.

Graham B, Zweig J. 2003. *The Intelligent Investor: The Definitive Book on Value Investing*. HarperCollins Publishers Inc.

Kahneman D, Tversky A. 1979. *Prospect Theory: An Analysis of Decision*. Scholarly Article. Econometrica

Kendall, Diana. 2008. *Sociology in our times*. Text Book. Thomson Wadsworth. Seventh Edition.

Lowenstein, Roger. 2001. *When Genius Failed: The Rise and Fall of Long-Term Capital Management*. Random House Inc.

Siegel, Jeremy. 2014. *Stocks for the Long Run: The Definitive Guide to Financial Market Returns & Long-Term Investment Strategies*. McGraw-Hill Education. Fifth Edition.

Thaler R, Johnson E. 1990. *Gambling with the House Money and Trying to Break Even: The Effects of Prior Outcomes on Risky Choice*. Scholarly Article. New York. Johnson Graduate School of Management, Cornell University.

Tzu, Sun. 2015. *The Art of War*. The Original Authoritative Edition. Translated by Lionel Giles. Wisehouse Publishing.

William, James. 2013. *On Vital Reserves: The Energies of Men; The Gospel of Relaxation*. Windham Press.

Appendix 12 – Recommended YouTube Personas

1.) Greg O'Gallagher – Kinobody – O'Gallagher explains intermittent fasting very well. If interested in intermittent fasting and relative strength targets I highly suggest his YouTube Channel: https://www.youtube.com/user/gog9

2.) Jeff Cavalier – Athlene X – Cavalier is a great source for workout exercises and really does live up to his mantra, "Putting The Science Back in Strength." If you want a highly functional athletic body I suggest checking out his channel: https://www.youtube.com/user/JDCav24

3.) Owen Cook – Real Social Dynamics (RSD) – Cook's material comes from the point of view of a "pick up artist". That being said, many of the core values I mention in this book correlate well with Cook's more universal concepts. This is because many of Owen's original material and ideas also stems from more renowned famous authors like Stephen Covey. While RSD has branded itself as a more sex orientated, "gamy", short term view, there can be no denying the overlap between the two intentions during the initial phases of relationships. Many of my journaled findings lend themselves well with Owen's more holistic ideas despite this divergence of intention. Therefore, despite this divergence, some of Owen's more holistic video ideas are recommended: https://www.youtube.com/user/RSDTyler

4.) Radu Antoniu – Think Eat Lift – Antoniu is a great source of health & body information. He conveys targeting body fat percentage with waist size extremely well. Radu is much more engaging than traditional book sources: https://www.youtube.com/user/raduantoniu

40567455R00141

Made in the USA
Middletown, DE
16 February 2017